GOD'S DICE

by **DAVID BADDIEL**

God's Dice was first performed on 24 October 2019 at
Soho Theatre, London, presented by Soho Theatre and Avalon.

GOD'S DICE
by DAVID BADDIEL

CAST

HENRY	Alan Davies
EDIE	Leila Mimmack
VIRGINIA	Alexandra Gilbreath
TIM	Nitin Ganatra
INTERLOCUTER and BILLY	Adam Strawford

CREATIVE TEAM AND PRODUCTION CREDITS

Director	James Grieve
Set and Costume Designer	Lucy Osborne
Lighting Designer	Ric Mountjoy
Sound Designer	Dominic Kennedy
Video Designer	Ash J Woodward
Casting Director	Nadine Rennie CDG
Costume Supervisor	Jackie Orton
Assistant Director	Sophie Drake
Production Manager	Seb Cannings for Gary Beestone Events & Theatre
Company Stage Manager	Anna Hunscott
Assistant Stage Manager	Amber Reece-Greenhalgh
Wardrobe Assistant	Clementine Curry
Produced by	Soho Theatre and Avalon
Producer	Emma Brünjes for Avalon
Producer	Alex Turner for Soho Theatre
Assistant Producer	Holly De Angelis
Marketing	JHI Marketing
Press and PR	Jo Allan PR
Scenic Builders	RT Scenery
Staging Hires	RK Resources
Lighting Hires	Sparks
Video Hires	Middlesex University and Blue-i

SPECIAL THANKS

Angela Di Tomaso, Sam Jeffs, Lamp & Pencil, Martin by HARMAN, Danni Reece-Greenhalgh, Ben Turnbull and David Tyler.

CAST

ALAN DAVIES | HENRY

Theatre credits include *Auntie and Me* (Wyndham's Theatre) and *The Odd Couple* (Assembly Rooms).

Film credits include *The Bromley Boys, Angus, Thongs and Perfect Snogging* and *Dog Eat Dog*.

Television credits include *Jonathan Creek, The Midnight Gang, Damned, Whites, The Brief, Bob and Rose, Roman Road, Hotel Babylon, Lewis, Good Housekeeping, Miss Marple* and *One for the Road*.

ALEXANDRA GILBREATH | VIRGINIA

Theatre credits include *The Provok'd Wife, Shakespeare Live, The Rover, Twelfth Night* – Olivier Award Nomination for Best Supporting Actress, *The Taming of the Shrew, RSC Big Birthday Bash, The Merry Wives of Windsor, The Tamer Tamed, Romeo and Juliet, As You Like It, The Winter's Tale, Cyrano de Bergerac, Love's Labour's Lost, The County Wife* and *Ghosts* (Royal Shakespeare Company), *The Village Bike* and *Disappeared* (Royal Court), *Dessert* (Southwark Playhouse), *Mother Christmas* (Hampstead Theatre), *The Lie* (Menier Chocolate Factory), *The Invisible* (Bush Theatre), *The War of the Roses* (Rose Theatre), *Playhouse Creatures* (Chichester Festival Theatre), *Othello* (Sheffield Theatres), *King Lear* (Leeds Playhouse), *Hedda Gabler* – Winner of the Ian Charleson Award (ETT and Donmar Warehouse) and *Shallow Slumber* (Soho Theatre).

Film credits include *A Hundred Streets, Tulip Fever, The All Together* and *Dead Babies*.

Television credits include *EastEnders, Monarch of the Glen, Casualty, Father Brown, Doctors, Inspector George Gently, Life Begins* and *The Bill*.

Alexandra is a Royal Shakespeare Company Associate Artist.

LEILA MIMMACK | EDIE

Theatre credits include *Richard III* (Headlong UK tour), *The Winter's Tale* and *To Kill a Mockingbird* (Bolton Octagon), *Debris* (Southwark Playhouse), *A View From the Bridge* (Royal Exchange), *That Face* (Sheffield Theatres) and *Sweeney Todd* and *Toad of Toad Hall* (Loft Theatre).

Film credits include *Level Up, High Rise, Son of God, The Sleeping Room, Game* and *Seamonsters*.

Television credits include *Love, Lies and Records, Homefires, Midwinter of the Spirit, Silent Witness, Law and Order, WPC 56, Frankie, Becoming Human, EastEnders* and *Married, Single, Other*.

NITIN GANATRA | TIM

Theatre credits include *End of the Pier* (Park Theatre), *Animal Farm* and *Skinflicks* (Belgrade Theatre), *As I Lay Dying* and *Twelfth Night* (Young Vic), *Blessings* (B&R Productions and The Old Red Lion), *D'yer Eat With Your Fingers?* (Stratford East), *Dice With the Devil* (Glynne Wickham Studio), *Haroun and the Sea of Stories* and *The Sanctuary* (National Theatre), *I Am Not India/Kiwi* (Southwark Playhouse), *Jungle Book* (MAC), *Kootle Mountain* (Candid Café), *Les Enfants Du Paradis* (Royal Shakespeare Company), *Listening Too Fast* (International tour), *Lucifer You...* and *Testimonial* (UK tour), *Macbeth* (Tricycle Theatre), *Oh Sweet Sita* (Tara Arts), *Parallel Lines* (Place Theatre), *The Bacchae* and *Turandot* (Edinburgh Festival), *To the Green Fields Beyond* (Donmar Warehouse), *Touched* (Might and Man Physical Theatre Company), *Twelfth Night* (Border Crossings) and *Wilder Shores of Live* (Battersea Arts Centre).

Film credits include *Hellboy: Rise of the Blood Queen*, *Eaten by Lions*, *Bride and Prejudice*, *Charlie and the Chocolate Factory*, *Chess*, *Colour Me Kubrick*, *Guru in Seven*, *Inferno*, *Mad, Bad & Sad*, *Mistress of Spices*, *Our Charley*, *Piccadilly Jim*, *Pure*, *Secrets and Lies*, *Shifty*, *Stag*, *The Drop*, *The Hunting Party*, *The Love Doctor*, *This Bastard Business* and *Truly, Madly, Deeply*.

Television credits include *The Worst Witch*, *Midsomer Murders*, *Silent Witness*, *Crossing the Border*, *Cornershop Superhero*, *Twenty Twelve*, *Being April*, *Canterbury Tales*, *EastEnders*, *England Expects*, *Extremely Dangerous*, *Hounded*, *Indian Dreams*, *Jane Hall's Big Bad Bus Ride*, *Kumbh Mela*, *Me and Mrs Jones*, *Meet the Magoons*, *Mumbai Calling* – Series 1, *Murder in Mind*, *New Street Law*, *New Tricks*, *Randall and Hopkirk*, *Rescue Me*, *Revenge*, *Second Generation*, *Shadow in the North*, *Silent Witness*, *Sins*, *Small Potatoes*, *Son of the Dragon*, *The Astronuts*, *The Bill*, *The Catherine Tate Christmas Special*, *The Grey Man*, *The Jury*, *The Real Deal*, *Thief Takers*, *This Life*, *Trial and Retribution*, *Twisted Tales: In at the Death*, *Welcome to Strathmore* and *You're Breaking Up*.

ADAM STRAWFORD | INTERLOCUTER AND BILLY

Theatre credits include *The Plough and the Stars* (Lyric Hammersmith and Abbey Theatre, Dublin) and *Romeo and Juliet* (Shakespeare in the Squares).

Film credits include *355*, *Faces* and *46*.

CREATIVE TEAM

DAVID BADDIEL | PLAYWRIGHT

David is a comedian, novelist and television presenter known for his work alongside Rob Newman in *The Mary Whitehouse Experience* and partnership with Frank Skinner. Besides comedy, he is a published novelist, screenwriter and author of children's novels *The Parent Agency*, *The Person Controller*, *AniMalcolm*, *Birthday Boy*, *Head Kid* and *The Taylor Turbocharger*. His critically acclaimed show *FAME: Not the Musical* ran at the Edinburgh Festival Fringe in 2013, transferring to London and subsequently touring the country. David's next one-man show, *My Family: Not the Sitcom*, premiered at London's Menier Chocolate Factory in 2016 before going on to run for 15 weeks in the West End, receive an Olivier Award nomination, and complete national and international tours. In 2020, David will be touring his new show, *Trolls: Not the Dolls*, across the UK.

JAMES GRIEVE | DIRECTOR

James was Joint Artistic Director of Paines Plough, the UK's national theatre of new plays, from 2010-2019. In his decade at the helm alongside George Perrin, Paines Plough produced 49 multi-award winning world premieres on tour to more than 300 places across the UK and internationally in spaces ranging from village halls and nightclubs to the National Theatre and Off-Broadway. In 2014 they launched Roundabout, the world's first pop-up plug-and-play theatre to tour new plays to underserved places. For Paines Plough, James directed new plays including *You Stupid Darkness!* by Sam Steiner, *Pop Music* by Anna Jordan, *Out of Love* by Elinor Cook, *Black Mountain* by Brad Birch, *How To Be a Kid* by Sarah McDonald Hughes, *Broken Biscuits* and *Jumpers For Goalposts* by Tom Wells, *Happiness* by Nick Payne (BBC Radio 3), *The Angry Brigade* by James Graham, *An Intervention* and *Love, Love, Love* by Mike Bartlett, *Hopelessly Devoted* and *Wasted* by Kate Tempest and *The Sound of Heavy Rain* by Penelope Skinner. His freelance work includes a new production of *Les Misérables* for Wermland Opera in Sweden, the new musical *The Assassination of Katie Hopkins* for Theatr Clwyd, which won Best Musical Production at the UK Theatre Awards 2018 and Brian Friel's *Translations*, which won Best Production at the UK Theatre Awards 2014. James was formerly co-founder and Artistic Director of nabokov and Associate Director at the Bush Theatre.

LUCY OSBORNE | SET AND COSTUME DESIGNER

Lucy's recent credits include *Rich Kids* (Traverse and UK tour), *The Assassination of Katie Hopkins* (Theatr Clwyd), *Rutherford and Son*, *One Flew Over the Cuckoo's Nest* (Sheffield Theatres), *Les Misérables* (Wermland Opera), *Uncle Vanya* (Theatr Clwyd and Sheffield Theatres) and *A Pacifist's Guide to The War on Cancer* (National Theatre and Complicité UK and Australia tour).

Forthcoming work includes a new production of *Cabaret* (Gothenburg Opera).

Lucy is a co-designer of Roundabout, the world's first flat-pack theatre and winner of The Stage Awards 'Theatre Building of the Year'. With her company studio three sixty Lucy creates pop-up performance venues and temporary installations. Their festival venue The Mix has featured at HighTide Festival of new writing and they are currently working with Wise Children to create a pop-up rehearsal room and with The Point in Eastleigh to renovate and reimagine a studio theatre and community space. studio three sixty recently designed the front of house areas for Wise Children's new show *Malory Towers* which was performed in a railway passenger shed in Bristol.

Lucy is a theatre consultant for Charcoalblue, advising on performance design and planning, and is currently working with the Institute of Contemporary Art (ICA) and the Royal Academy of Dance in London.

RIC MOUNTJOY | LIGHTING DESIGNER

Ric designs lighting for theatre and opera, and his work has been seen all over the world, including the Singapore International Arts Festival; in Seattle, Dubai, Bahrain and Doha; Hong Kong, Seoul, Guangzhou and Beijing, and most significantly in London and New York City.

Recent credits include *The Play That Goes Wrong* on Broadway (Lyceum Theatre), on a US national tour (2018–2020), in the West End (Duchess Theatre – winner of the 2015 Olivier Award for Best New Comedy), in Australia, in South Korea, *Uncle Vanya* (Theatr Clwyd and Sheffield Theatres), *Darbar Festival* (Akram Khan Company and Sadler's Wells), *Emancipation of Expressionism* (Boy Blue Entertainment, Barbican Theatre and BBC TV), *Little Mermaid* (Theatre Royal Bath), *Mr Popper's Penguins* (Seattle, Minneapolis, New York City and West End), a site-specific *The Great Gatsby* (Guild of Misrule and Theatr Clwyd), the site-specific world premiere of *Karagula* by Philip Ridley (DEM and Soho Theatre), *What the Ladybird Heard* (West End and international tours) and *Bunny* (Edinburgh, London and New York – Fringe First Award). He lights site-specific theatre for the company Slung Low, including *The White Whale* – an outdoor adaptation of *Moby Dick* (Leeds), *Pandemic* (Singapore), *Anthology* (Liverpool Everyman) and *Beyond the Frontline* (The Lowry).

Associate Lighting Designer credits include *The Magic Flute* (London Coliseum, ENO) and *The Angry Brigade* (Paines Plough and Bush Theatre).

Ric worked for many years at English National Opera, and before that for Birmingham Royal Ballet.

DOMINIC KENNEDY | SOUND DESIGNER

Dominic is a sound designer and music producer for performance and live events; he has a keen interest in developing new work and implementing sound and music at an early stage in a creative process. Dominic is a graduate from the Royal Central School of Speech and Drama. He has developed specialist skills in collaborative and devised theatre making, music composition and installation practices. His work often fuses found sound, field recordings, music composition and synthesis.

Recent credits include *A History of Water in the Middle East* (Royal Court), *Lit* (Nottingham Playhouse), Roundabout Season 2019 (Paines Plough), *You Stupid Darkness!* (Paines Plough and Theatre Royal Plymouth), *Pop Music* (Paines Plough, Birmingham REP and Latitude), *Skate Hard Turn Left* (Battersea Arts Centre), Roundabout Season 2018 (Paines Plough and Theatr Clwyd), *Angry Alan* (Soho Theatre), *The Assassination of Katie Hopkins* (Theatr Clwyd), *With a Little Bit of Luck* (Paines Plough and BBC Radio 1Xtra), *Ramona Tells Jim* (Bush Theatre), *And the Rest of Me Floats* (Outbox), *I Am A Tree* (Jamie Wood) and *Box Clever* (nabokov).

ASH J WOODWARD | VIDEO DESIGNER

Ash specialises in video and projection design for live performance. He has designed and animated content for large scale shows in the West End and on Broadway, as well as smaller fringe and scratch performances all over the world. Ash has won a Drama Desk Award, OCC Award and a WhatsOnStage Award for his video design.

Recent credits include *Harry Potter and the Cursed Child* (London, New York, Melbourne, San Francisco and Hamburg), *Armadillo* (Yard Theatre), *The Cunning Little Vixen* (Royal Opera House), *The Divide* (The Old Vic) and *Molly* (Squint and Edinburgh Festival).

Non-theatre credits include *Bletchley Park: Hut 11A* (Bletchley Park), *You Say You Want a Revolution* (V&A), *Years & Years* (UK tour), Jess Glynne Arena Tour (UK tour) and the Rolling Stones exhibit *Exhibitionism* (Saatchi Gallery).

NADINE RENNIE CDG | CASTING DIRECTOR

Nadine was in-house Casting Director at Soho Theatre for fifteen years, working on new plays by writers including Dennis Kelly, Bryony Lavery, Arinzé Kene, Roy Williams, Philip Ridley, Laura Wade and Vicky Jones.

Since going freelance in January 2019, Nadine has worked for Arcola Theatre (*HOARD* and *The Glass Menagerie*), Tiata Fahodzi (*Good Dog*), Orange Tree Theatre (*Little Baby Jesus*), Sheffield Crucible (*The Last King of Scotland*), Leeds Playhouse (*There Are No Beginnings* and *Random*), Fuel Theatre (*The Little Prince*), National Theatre of Wales (*Price*) and continues to cast for Soho Theatre (most recently *Typical* and *Shuck 'n' Jive*).

Her TV work includes casting the first three series of CBBC's BAFTA-winning *Dixi*.

Nadine also has a long-running association as Casting Director for Synergy Theatre Project and is a member of the Casting Directors Guild.

JACKIE ORTON | COSTUME SUPERVISOR

Jackie was Deputy Head of Costume at the Royal Court Theatre for 12 years under Dominic Cooke and Ian Rickson. During that time she supervised many shows including *Posh, Jumpy* and *Clybourne Park*, all of which transferred to the West End. Other Royal Court shows include *The Low Road, Sucker Punch, Chicken Soup with Barley, The Pride* and *The Girlfriend Experience* (also Young Vic).

Recent credits include *The Bee* and *Dandy in The Underworld* (Soho Theatre), *Dusty The Musical* (UK tour), *The Two Noble Kinsmen, Salome, Duchess of Malfi, Troilus and Cressida, As You Like It* and *King John* (Royal Shakespeare Company), *The Jungle* (Young Vic), *Lady Windermere's Fan* (Vaudeville Theatre), *Everybody's Talking About Jamie* (Sheffield Theatres and Apollo Theatre), *Cat on a Hot Tin Roof* (Apollo Theatre), *Who's Afraid of Virginia Woolf* (Harold Pinter Theatre), *Henry V* (Open Air Theatre), *A Christmas Carol* (Noël Coward Theatre), *The Hairy Ape, High Society* and *The Crucible* (The Old Vic), *The Father* (Ustinov Studio Bath, Tricycle and West End), *Di and Viv and Rose* (Hampstead Theatre and West End), *East is East* (Trafalgar Studios and UK tour) and *Little Revolution* (Almeida Theatre).

SOPHIE DRAKE | ASSISTANT DIRECTOR

Sophie trained at the University of Leeds and is the Resident Director for Broken Silence Theatre Company.

Direction credits include *Post* (Old Red Lion), *My Boys* (Theatre503), *Constellations* (Hen & Chickens Theatre and Banham Theatre), *Colin McKenzie* (Greenside) and *NSFW* (Schonell Theatre).

Assistant and associate direction credits include *The Weatherman* (Park Theatre), *Notice* as part of *The Miniaturists* (Arcola Theatre), *In Lipstick* (Pleasance Theatre), *A Sticky Season* (Tristan Bates Theatre), *Maggie May* and *Homos, or Everyone in America* (Finborough Theatre).

Trainee direction credits includes *Red* (Wyndham's Theatre).

SEB CANNINGS | PRODUCTION MANAGER FOR GARY BEESTONE EVENTS & THEATRE

A graduate of the Royal Central School of Speech and Drama, Seb joined Gary Beestone Events & Theatre as Assistant Production Manager for *Harry Potter and the Cursed Child*. Now supporting all areas of the business, Seb is Production Manager for a range of projects and his recent credits include *Snow White* (London Palladium), *Blueberry Toast* and *The One* (Soho Theatre), *The Entertainer* (UK tour), *Puma Future Vault* (Urban Nerds), Hull City of Culture and *Wilde Creatures* (Tall Stories).

His client list includes Soho Theatre, Kenny Wax, Qdos, Tall Stories, Oxford Playhouse, Cambridge Arts Theatre and Simon Friend Entertainment.

EMMA BRÜNJES | PRODUCER FOR AVALON

Emma founded ebp, Emma Brünjes Productions, in 2013. ebp is a live entertainment company specialising in Production, General Management and Talent Management. The company has produced and created multiple productions across the UK and internationally.

ebp was nominated for an Olivier Award in 2016 for *Alice's Adventures Underground*, and the Innovation award at The Stage Awards 2017. Emma was listed in *The Stage*'s 100 Power List and The Hospital 100 Club Awards.

Prior to ebp Emma was General Manager of Productions and Programming at Nimax Theatres having been invited to join Nica Burns after six years at Avalon Entertainment.

Emma is a board member for Stage One and the League of Independent Producers, Producer of Dave's Edinburgh Comedy Awards and a member of the Society of London Theatre.

ALEX TURNER | PRODUCER FOR SOHO THEATRE

Alex's recent Producer and General Manager credits include *Gently Down the Stream* (Park Theatre – Olivier Award nomination for Outstanding Achievement in an Affiliate Theatre), *Homos, or Everyone in America* and *Adding Machine: A Musical* (Finborough Theatre), *One Arm* (Southwark Playhouse – Off West End Award for Best Director) and, currently, *A Prayer for Wings* (King's Head Theatre) and *Clybourne Park* (Park Theatre).

His career has spanned producing major premieres and revivals of plays and musicals at theatres including Sheffield Theatres and the Bush Theatre, as Interim Producer for both; project management, including TheatreCraft 2018, the UK's largest theatre careers event; and working on the general management of internationally acclaimed plays and musicals at Playful Productions, including *The Audience* starring Kristin Scott Thomas, the West End premiere of *Kinky Boots, No Man's Land* starring Ian McKellen and Patrick Stewart, *Don Juan in Soho* starring David Tennant and *Lady Day at Emerson's Bar & Grill* starring Audra McDonald, where he also worked on the development of new work for the company. He has also worked as a co-founding Artist and Producer of non zero one, with whom he devised interactive theatre productions for the Barbican, National Theatre, Bush Theatre, Science Museum and Edinburgh Fringe, taught courses on the Undergraduate Drama and Theatre degree at Royal Holloway, University of London, and worked as a publicist with Kate Morley PR and the Royal Shakespeare Company.

Soho Theatre is London's most vibrant venue for new theatre, comedy and cabaret with a national and international touring programme, a digital presence and an additional venue in progress. As entrepreneurial as we are innovative, under the leadership of Executive Director Mark Godfrey and Creative Director David Luff, our charity and social enterprise's mission is to produce new work, discover and nurture new writers and artists, and target and develop new audiences.

We work with artists in a variety of ways, from full producing of new plays, to co-producing new work, working with associate artists and presenting the best new emerging theatre companies that we can find.

We have numerous artists on attachment and under commission, including Soho Six and a thriving Company of writers and comedy groups. We read and see hundreds of scripts and shows a year.

'The place was buzzing, and there were queues all over the building as audiences waited to go into one or other of the venue's spaces... exuberant and clearly anticipating a good time.' *Guardian*

We attract over 240,000 audience members a year at Soho Theatre, at festivals and through our national and international touring. We produced, co-produced or staged over 40 new plays in the last 12 months.

As an entrepreneurial charity and social enterprise, we have created an innovative and sustainable business model. We maximise value from Arts Council England and philanthropic funding, contributing more to government in tax and NI than we receive in public funding.

sohotheatre.com
@sohotheatre all social media

Registered Charity No: 267234

Soho Theatre, 21 Dean Street
London W1D 3NE
Admin 020 7287 5060
Box Office 020 7478 0100

AVALON

Founded in 1989, by Jon Thoday and Richard Allen-Turner, Avalon has offices in the UK and the USA, and is a multi-award-winning talent management, live promotion and television production group.

The company's talent management arm has discovered countless acts who have become household names. Those represented include Chris Addison, David Baddiel, Adrian Chiles, Greg Davies, Rob Delaney, Adam Devine, Jenny Eclair, Dave Gorman, Freddie Highmore, Alex Horne, Russell Howard, Toby Jones, Lee Mack, Leslie Manville, Mark Maron, Rose Matafeo, Al Murray, James Nesbitt, John Oliver, Daniel Radcliffe, Frank Skinner and Imelda Staunton.

Avalon Television is the UK's top 'true independent' television production company and has produced numerous ground-breaking television shows including Emmy and Peabody award-winner *Last Week Tonight* with John Oliver (HBO), Emmy-nominated *Catastrophe* (Channel 4/Amazon Prime), RTS and Rose d'Or winning *Not Going Out* (BBC1's longest-running sitcom currently on air), multi-BAFTA award winning *Harry Hill's TV Burp* (ITV1), *Taskmaster* (DAVE/Comedy Central US), *Russell Howard's Good News* (BBC2), *Fantasy Football League* (BBC/ITV), *The Frank Skinner Show* (ITV) and *Workaholics* (Comedy Central USA).

Outside of television, the company's live arm has produced the most nominees of the Edinburgh Comedy Awards of all time, as well as producing *Newman and Baddiel: Live at Wembley*, the first ever arena comedy show in British history. Further notable work includes *Jerry Springer: The Opera* (National Theatre, Cambridge Theatre and 2006 National UK tour) by Richard Thomas and Stewart Lee, the first West End show to win all four Best New Musical awards and countless major live shows and national and international tours.

avalonuk.com

OPPORTUNITIES FOR WRITERS
AT SOHO THEATRE

We are looking for unique and unheard voices – from all backgrounds, attitudes and places.

We want to make things you've never seen before.

Alongside workshops, readings and notes sessions, there are several ways writers can connect with Soho Theatre. You can

Enter our prestigious biennial competition the Verity Bargate Award just as Vicky Jones did in 2013 with her award-winning first play *The One*.

Participate in our nine-month-long Writers' Labs programme, where we will take you through a three-draft process.

Submit your script to submissions@sohotheatre.com where your play will go directly to our Artistic team.

Invite us to see your show via coverage@sohotheatre.com

We consider every submission for production or any of the further development opportunities.

sohotheatre.com

SUPPORTERS

Principal Supporters
Nicholas Allott OBE
Hani Farsi
Hedley and Fiona
  Goldberg
Michael and Isobel
  Holland
Jack and Linda Keenan
Amelia and Neil Mendoza
Lady Susie Sainsbury
Carolyn Ward
Jennifer and Roger
  Wingate

Supporting Partners
Dean Attew
Jo Bennett-Coles
Tamara Box
Matthew Bunting
Stephen Garrett
Beatrice Hollond
Angela Hyde-Courtney
Ian Mill
Phil & Jane Radcliff
Dom & Ali Wallis
Garry Watts

Corporate Supporters
Adnams Southwold
Bargate Murray
Bates Wells & Braithwaite
Cameron Mackintosh Ltd
Character Seven
EPIC Private Equity
Financial Express
Fosters
The Groucho Club
John Lewis Oxford Street
Latham & Watkins LLP
Lionsgate UK
The Nadler Hotel
Oberon Books Ltd
Overbury Leisure
Quo Vardis
Richmond Associates
Soho Estates
Soundcraft

Trusts & Foundations
The 29th May 1961
  Charitable Trust
The Andor Charitable
  Trust
Backstage Trust
Bertha Foundation
Bruce Wake Charitable
  Trust
The Boris Karloff
  Charitable Foundation
The Boshier-Hinton
  Foundation

The Buzzacott Stuart
  Defries Memorial Fund
Chapman Charitable Trust
The Charles Rifkind and
  Jonathan Levy
  Charitable Settlement
The Charlotte Bonham-
  Carter Charitable Trust
Cockayne – Grants for the
  Arts and The London
  Community Foundation
John S Cohen Foundation
The Coutts Charitable
  Trust
The David and Elaine
  Potter Foundation
The D'Oyly Carte
  Charitable Trust
The Eranda Rothschild
  Foundation
The Ernest Cook Trust
Esmée Fairbairn
  Foundation
The Fenton Arts Trust
Fidelio Charitable Trust
The Foundation for Sport
  and the Arts
Foyle Foundation
Garrick Charitable Trust
The Goldsmiths'
  Company
The Late Mrs Margaret
  Guido's Charitable
  Trust
Harold Hyam Wingate
  Foundation
Hyde Park Place Estate
  Charity
The Ian Mactaggart Trust
The Idlewild Trust
The John Thaw
  Foundation
John Ellerman
  Foundation
John Lewis Oxford Street
  Community Matters
  Scheme
John Lyon's Charity
JP Getty Jnr Charitable
  Trust
The Kobler Trust
The Leche Trust
The Mackintosh
  Foundation
Mohamed S. Farsi
  Foundation
Noël Coward Foundation
The Peggy Ramsay
  Foundation
The Rose Foundation
The Royal Victoria Hall
  Foundation
Santander Foundation

Schroder Charity Trust
St Giles-in-the-Fields and
  William Shelton
  Educational Charity
The St James's Piccadilly
  Charity
Tallow Chandlers
  Benevolent Fund
The Teale Charitable Trust
The Theatres Trust
The Thistle Trust
Unity Theatre Charitable
  Trust
The Wolfson Foundation

**Soho Theatre
Performance Friends**
Rajan Brotia
Alban Gordon
Joe Lam
Andrew Lucas
Walter Ken McCracken
  and Stacie Styles
Mark Whiteley
Gary Wilder

**Soho Theatre
Playwright Friends**
David Aukin
Quentin Bargate
Emily Fletcher
Liam Goddard
Fawn James
John James
Shappi Khorsandi
Jeremy King OBE
David and Linda Lakhdhir
Susie Lea
Jonathan Levy
Nick & Annette Mason
Suki Sanhdu OBE
Lesley Symons
Henry Wyndham
Christopher Yu

**Soho Theatre
Comedy Friends**
Kerry Abel
Tiffany Agbeko
Oladipo Agboluaje
Rachel Agustsson
Fran Allen
Matthew Allen
Katherine Andreen
Robert Ash
Adele Ashton
James Atkinson
Valentine Attew
Gabrielle Baigel
Polly Balsom
John Bannister
Patrick Barrett
Zarina Bart
Uri Baruchin
Antonio Batista

Ben Battcock
David Baynard
Elaine Becker
David Bend
Alex Bertulis-Fernandes
Julia Biro
Sophie Birshan
Kieran Birt
Matthew Boyle
Christian Braeker
Jesse Buckle
Iain Burnett
Oscar Cainer
Lynsey Campbell
Indigo Carnie
Chris Carter
Deborah Charles
Nicholas Clemmow
Camilla Cole
Vanessa Cook
Grant Court
Eva Culhane
Alli Cunningham
Josephine Curry
Mark David
Haralambos Dayantis
Sharon Eva Degen
Laura Denholm
Jeff Dormer
Edwina Ellis
Kate Emery
Samantha Fennessy
Peter Fenwick
Stephen Ferns
Sue Fletcher
Stephen Fowler
Kevin French
Paul Friedman
John Fry
David Gardner
Cyrus Gilbert-Rolfe
Cindy Glenn
Jake Godfrey
Kiera Godfrey
Terry Good
Robert Grant
Steven Greenwood
Emma Gunnell
Edward Hacking
Gary Haigh
John Hamilton
Colin Hann
Anthony Hawser
Simon Herman
Karen Howlett
Georgia Ince
John Ireland
Nadia Jennings
Clodagh de Jode
Simon Jones
Sue Jones

Toby Jones
Amelia Kenworthy
David King
Robert King
Hari Kitching
Julie Knight
Eric Knopp
Andreas Kubat
Michael Kunz
Emily Kyne
Clive Laing
Philip Lawson
Simon Lee
Damien Lefortier
Kerry Jean Lister
Ian Livingston
Lucy Lumsden
Lucy MacCarthy
Jane Maguire
Marea Maloney
Anthony Marraccino
Amanda Mason
Douglas McIlroy
Lauren McLardie
Paul McNamee
Chris McQuiggin
Jennifer Meech
Laura Meecham
Kosten Metreweli
Mike Miller
Nick Mills
Nathan Mosher
Maryam Mossavar
Jim Murgatroyd
Mr and Mrs Roger
   Myddelton
Bianca Nardi
Lena Nguyen
James Nicoll
John O'Keeffe
Samantha O'Sullivan
Alan Pardoe
Simon Parsonage
Helen Pegrum
Curro Perez Alcantara
Andrew Perkins
Keith Petts
Marijn Poeschmann
Nick Pontt
Helena Prytz
Stephanie Ressort
Annabel Ridley
Giles Robinette
Antonia Rolph
Dan Rosenberg
Kate Ross
Graeme Rossiter
Tamanna Ruparel
Lauren Rutherford
Rebecca Rycroft
Benjamin Samuel

Ron Sandler
Natalia Siabkin
Beth Silver
Michelle Singer
Amanda Singleton
Christopher Slevin
Hari Sriskantha
Sarah Stanford
Tom Stockton
Jennifer Stott
Dorota Strak
Barry Street
Christine Styrnau
Catherine Taite
Tracey Tattersall
Daniel Taylor
Sarah Taylor
Victoria Thomas
Andrew Thorne
Anthony Stewart Townson
Domenico Veronese
Rocco Vogel
Gabriel Vogt
Elizabeth Vrachimi
Trent Walton
Toby Warren
Zachary Webb
Sam Webster
Mike Welsh
Matt Whitehurst
Luke Wiles
Alexandra Williams
Gareth Williams
Geoff Williams
Kevin Williams
Sion Williams-Eliyesil
Allan Willis
Diana Wilson
Jennifer Wood
Anna Woolgar
Neil Woollard
Laura Wright
Liz Young

We are also supported by
Westminster City Council
West End Ward Budget
and the London Borough
of Waltham Forest.
We would also like to
thank those supporters
who wish to remain
anonymous

INTRODUCTION

My dad was a scientist – still is, even through the fog of dementia (if you ask him what the chemical formula for salt is, he'll still shout NACKL!, a my-dad word for NaCl, or sodium chloride). I'm not. I was going to be – I had chosen Chemistry, Physics and Maths A levels – but that was because, in our family, because of my dad, science was King: no other form of intellectual endeavor was considered of any value. Luckily for me, and the scientific world, I realised at the last minute that regularly getting Ds and Es in science subjects, whilst doing considerably better in arts and humanities, meant that I should focus on those. When I, with some trepidation, told my dad, he said: 'It's a waste of a brain.' Hmm. But then anyone who saw my last theatrical outing, my one-man show *My Family: Not the Sitcom* will know that what we would now call 'parenting' was not his strong point.

Anyway: unlike Luke Skywalker, I am not my father's son. I think watching, or indeed writing, books and plays and films is not a waste of a brain. But something must have stuck, or some return of the repressed is happening. Because as I get older I've found myself reading, amongst all the novels and plays, a lot of science books. Not proper ones, obviously, the sort that students have to plough through at university, but the popular kind – by Brian Cox and Carlo Rovelli and Brian Greene. Ones that do their best, for those of us who can hardly add up the price of their weekly shop, to explain the mysteries of modern physics without mathematics.

The correct equation is probably my father plus mortality. As you get older, you see your time left to understand what the universe is truly about narrowing, and a part of me – my father – suspects that the only real understanding lies in science. Specifically, quantum physics: because there is something about looking deep into the microscopic heart of things that surely – almost banally – will give you that answer. We are visual animals, and we think if we peer deep enough, we will always crack mystery.

Wrong, of course. I noticed that, however much I read, I never quite understood. Sometimes I would get close only for the sliver of understanding to vanish with a turn of the page and a new analogy involving clocks or ripples in a pond. Richard Feynman, one of those who looked very deeply into this mystery, said 'I think I can safely say that nobody understands quantum mechanics.' Even a smattering of knowledge of quantum physics will very quickly lead you to the conclusion that, the more you look, the less you understand. At the microscopic heart of things, mystery is not cracked: there is just more mystery. In fact, there is more than mystery, there is stuff that feels completely strange and weird and… well, miraculous. Which means that when scientists tell us: 'Sorry, that IS the way things are – we can't really explain it, you're just going to have to accept it – you're simply going to have to believe us' – it rang, for me, a familiar bell: a church one.

Or a mosque/synagogue/Zoroastrian Fire Temple one (yes I know they probably don't have bells…). In the realm of quantum physics, scientists seem to me to be like medieval priests. They have the obscure difficult language that only they understand – maths – and they are tasked with conveying the fundamental truths of the universe this language reveals to them back to the rest of us, using analogies and stories and reassurance. We have to have faith in this science, that tells us that everything we think we apprehend is something else entirely; that all we see is as through a glass, darkly, even if that glass is the lens of an electron microscope. Or at least that's how it felt to me, reading these books. Without a deep understanding of mathematics, there comes a point where you have to trust the wise ones. There comes a point, in other words, where you have to make a leap of faith.

The realisation that these two great shards of thought cross over in a Venn diagram involving faith, mystery, the miraculous, and a questioning of apparent reality brought me to thinking about the world we live in now, how much we seem to be in a time of desperate believing, but with less and less sense that what is believed is necessarily true. Truth has got very mixed up, it seems, with desire… so, anyway, I decided to try and write a play about all this, in which all those big concerns bang up against some more mundane faiths, the ones that sustain us from day to day: in love and marriage and friendship and the value of teaching and knowing one's place in the world. I hope you enjoy it. And that you close these pages thinking that I haven't, in the end, completely wasted my brain.

David Baddiel
October 2019

GOD'S DICE

David Baddiel

Characters

HENRY, *fifties*
EDIE, *twenties*
VIRGINIA, *forties*
TIM, *fifties*
BILLY, *twenties*

This text went to press before the end of rehearsals and so may differ slightly from the play as performed.

ACT ONE

Darkness: Music. The guitar chords of a slow acoustic version of 'Do Anything You Wanna Do' by Eddie & The Hot Rods. Bring up slowly the sounds of students arriving at a lecture hall.

Lights up. A lecture hall at a redbrick university. It is Exeter, but it could be any.

Behind a lectern, surveying his students (who figure here as the audience) is a lecturer, with a friendly demeanour: HENRY BROOK, *fifty. Next to him on the lectern is a glass of water.*

There are a number of laptops dotted around the stage, with the screens up, facing the audience. At present they all show a screensaver of Exeter University.

Behind HENRY *is a whiteboard, divided into two sections by a line down the middle. This needs to be a usuable whiteboard – i.e. writeable on – and available for projecting.*

On the left-hand section is a series of complex equations. It includes '$\Delta T = Time$' at the top.

Above the left-hand section, the words: 'The sorts of equations that appear on whiteboards in biopics about scientists'.

On the right-hand section: 'UNDERSTANDING PHYSICS'. HENRY *underlines it.*

He turns. Half-smiles.

HENRY. So. Who here would like to win the lottery?

    Beat.

    No one? I'm going to assume that's just shyness in a group of new students. I'm going to assume we all *would* like that. How do we *make* that happen? How do we without any shadow of doubt, win the lottery? There is one absolute way.

    Beat.

Kill yourself.

Beat, enjoying the effect.

I should be clear – I don't advise actually *doing* this. It's fraught with problems. You might get it wrong and end up horrifically injured. Plus, more importantly, you have to have a *lot* of faith – for want of a better word – in the idea of the many-worlds universe. But let's assume we do have that faith. Let's assume – just for a laugh – that the universe is indeed infinite, and anything that can happen, will happen. If you do, winning the lottery is very simple.

He goes over to the whiteboard. Talks, as he rubs off what's on there.

Firstly, you have to buy a lottery ticket. Let's say the numbers on your ticket are – let's make this easy – one two three four five – and a bonus ball: six.

Writes those numbers on the board.

Then what you have to do is go to bed before *The National Lottery In It To Win It* – or whatever it's called now – is on. On top of your bed – bit tricky, this bit – you have to construct some kind of device plugged into your TV, that if these numbers do *not* come up, including the bonus ball, will kill you.

He draws a version of what he's talking of.

Perhaps a ten-tonne anvil held in a magnetic field above your bed that responds to Alan Dedicoat's voice. Who knows? It's not important. What is important is that – even though you'll almost definitely be killed in this world, and most of the others in the multiverse – in *one* of the many worlds – these numbers *will* come up. In an infinite universe, they must do, somewhere. In fact, since the chances of winning the lottery on any normal week are in fact one in thirteen million, nine hundred and eighty-three thousand, eight hundred and sixteen, you won't even be killed in *that* many worlds. You'll be killed, to be exact, in thirteen million, nine hundred and eighty-three thousand, eight hundred and *fifteen* worlds. But in the thirteen million, nine hundred and eighty-three

thousand and eight hundred and *sixteenth*, you'll wake up –
alive and rich beyond your wildest dreams. How about that?

Sound of class shutting books, coughing, etc. HENRY *checks
his watch.*

So, look, not everything in my lectures is going to be *that*
exciting. But I thought I'd start you off with something that
made you think physics isn't going to be dull. And therefore
that you'd made the right choice for a degree. Google
Everett, many-universe theory and the Dirac delta function,
and we'll talk again tomorrow.

*Sound of chairs moving back, many students getting up,
leaving, a door opening, etc.* HENRY *starts wiping the
whiteboard.*

One student, EDIE, *appears from the wings. She watches his
back for a beat.*

EDIE. Professor Brook?

HENRY. Yes?

EDIE. Can I ask you a question?

HENRY. Of course.

EDIE. It's quite a long question.

This makes him look at her; and take an interest.

HENRY. Well, as long as I can still make it home in time for
dinner…

*She nods; she is self-serious, gives no indication of
flirtatiousness.*

EDIE (*deep breath*). I'm a Christian.

HENRY. Ah.

EDIE. I thought that's what you'd say.

HENRY. You thought I'd say Ah?

EDIE. Yes. Well, not exactly. I thought that would be your
attitude. Ah-ish.

HENRY. Ah-ish…

EDIE. As in 'Ah… she's a loony.' Or 'Ah… now I shan't take her seriously.'

HENRY. Right. Sorry…?

EDIE. Edie Eliot. I'm a first-year.

HENRY. In mathematical physics…?

EDIE. Yes. That had an element of Ah-ness to it too.

HENRY. What did?

EDIE. The way you said mathematical physics. With a sense of surprise. Despite the fact that I'm at one of your lectures. So likely to be studying your subject. You're surprised because I'm a Christian studying science.

HENRY (*shaking his head*). I've heard all about you Christian Scientists.

EDIE *smiles patiently at the joke*.

So. Edie. What was your question?

EDIE. Sorry, yes. Sorry. It's… Well. We could take anything from quantum mechanics as an example, but let's take: spin.

HENRY. Of subatomic particles?

EDIE. Yes.

HENRY. Okay. You understand that it's not spin as we imagine it in the everyday universe. The electron, for example, is *not* moving like a top.

EDIE. No, of course. The electron is spinning in all possible directions. At once. Only at the point of measurement, of observation, can it be said to be spinning in a particular direction.

HENRY. Yes, you *are* doing my subject. Very good.

EDIE. But actually for the purposes of the question, let's imagine that the spin of an electron is indeed like the spin of a top. I think it makes no difference to what I'm asking.

HENRY (*checks watch*). And what *are* you asking, exactly?

EDIE (*after a beat*). If you pair, say, an electron with another
electron –

HENRY. Quantum entanglement…

EDIE. Yes – if you entangle two electrons and then separate
them – *really* separate them – take electron B and shoot it
two hundred light years away from electron A… and then
you measure electron A, the one you've kept at home in your
lab, and find it's spinning one way…

HENRY. Yes…

EDIE.…then the one that's two hundred light years away – that
will instantaneously turn out to be spinning, will it not, in the
opposite direction? To stick with the 'top' metaphor, if
electron A is measured as spinning this way…

Spins her right finger clockwise, big circle.

…two-hundred-lights-years-away electron B which had been
going any which way…

Spins left-hand finger in general motions.

…will – *instantaneously* – be found to be going this way…

Left finger suddenly spins smoothly, anticlockwise.

She looks up from her fingers, both sticking up. HENRY
stares at her.

HENRY. Well. We can only *demonstrate* it using smaller
distances obviously. But for an electron, from here to Exeter
Cathedral is effectively two hundred light years away. So all
our mathematics would suggest that yes, even if you put two
hundred light years between them, at the point of
measurement, an electron – or indeed any other subatomic
particle, twinned with another will spin 'up' if its twin spins
'down' and vice versa. It's a phenomenon that Einstein
called spooky action at a distance. Is that your question?

EDIE. No. My question is: if you're truly asking me to believe
that – I may as well believe in God.

Beat.

Mightn't I?

Beat. HENRY *frowns. Makes to answer. But then doesn't.*

Blackout. Music. The main screen/whiteboard, plus the laptops, play a montage of atomic/subatomic fractals and patterns.

Lights up on HENRY*'s tasteful living room.* VIRGINIA *is seated with a glass of red wine. She has a laptop open on a US airlines site.* HENRY *is by a breakfast bar. He is kneading dough. A laptop is open with the words 'Bake Your Own Bread'.*

She is looking at him sharply. Beat.

VIRGINIA (*with some weight*). Edie…

HENRY. Yes. Sorry. What's her name got to do with it?

VIRGINIA. The fact that you remembered it. Most of your students figure in your memory as… Oh, y'know, V, the one with hair like *Eraserhead*. The one who might be dead. The one who smells of Cornish pasties.

HENRY (*laughing*). Yeah, he really did. Steak-and-kidney ones. From Greggs.

(*Looks at recipe.*) Have we got any cornmeal? What even is cornmeal?

VIRGINIA. Yes, funnily enough, it was a he. It tends to be the hes that you can't remember the names of.

HENRY. I just thought it was an interesting question, okay?

VIRGINIA. Oh no. Please, Henry, darling, please, please – don't start believing in God.

HENRY. Oh Virginia. Don't be so ridiculous! I'm a scientist!

VIRGINIA. I think it bothers me more than you getting all moon-eyed over some eighteen-year-old. That's what fifty-year-old men do.

HENRY. A – My eyes are completely un-moony, and B – She's twenty-three. She took some time off between school and university…

VIRGINIA. Oh, sorry. Twenty-three. I didn't realise. An old maid.

HENRY (*laughing*). I thought her question was interesting: not because it made the clouds part and the Lord waft me up to his bosom in his infinitely gentle hand, but because it offered a way of thinking about the imaginative impossibility of quantum physics.

VIRGINIA. All I'm really hearing there is the word bosom…

HENRY. Because: we can't truly imagine, not physically, what's going on in the subatomic world, just like we can't physically imagine, y'know, God.

VIRGINIA. That's because he doesn't exist.

HENRY. I know that. That's not even worth discussing. Certainly not in this house. But come with me, V. Just for a second. Intellectually.

Beat. She sighs.

VIRGINIA. I have come with you. I get your point. God, beyond our normal understanding. Quantum physics, likewise. Except: God is *not* beyond our understanding. The psychological reasons why we made him up are apparent. Have you not read any of my books?

HENRY. Of course. All of them. I'm a good husband.

VIRGINIA. Sometimes. Not when you come home with the news that a female student may have made you see the light…!

HENRY. I meant it ironically!

VIRGINIA. That's what men have been saying as an excuse for everything since 1993!

HENRY laughs, shakes his head, starts whacking dough about vigorously.

What are you doing?

HENRY. Trying to get a slightly fluffier crumb!

She laughs. He gives up the bread – picks up a glass, goes over to her with it, pours her more red wine.

VIRGINIA. Oh well. Just so long as while I'm in America, you don't join an Alpha Group. I won't be able to do my TED Talk for worrying about it…

HENRY. Sorry. I shouldn't have mentioned it. But you know, married couples – sitting down, having a drink, after work – they talk about their day. And my day – certainly telling *you* about it – you know – compared to some of the days *you* have… well, it can feel like there's nothing to tell.

VIRGINIA. Henry…

HENRY. Like today, for example. Apart from that conversation, with, yes, Edie… I answered emails, I listened to Tim complain about how Exeter is the worst university in Britain because it still hasn't offered him a permanent contract. I marked twenty-two third-year worksheets on Pauli spin matrices, most of which demonstrated that they hadn't understood a word I'd taught them during their first and second years. *And* I sat through a lunchtime meeting about '*personal development within performance review*' most of which I didn't understand, and I *do* understand Pauli spin matrices.

VIRGINIA. Well. That all sounds… very interesting.

HENRY. No it doesn't. That's the problem. You don't want to hear about my day. *I* don't even want to hear about my day.

VIRGINIA *laughs*.

So when something out of the ordinary *does* happen – like a student actually asks an out-of-the-ordinary question – it's a big deal. It's exciting. And when an exciting thing happens – even a tiny little thing — what's my first thought? Still? After twenty-three years?

He comes closer to her.

I must tell Virginia. I must know what V thinks of this.

Beat. She looks at him with love. Kisses him, gently.

VIRGINIA. You're so sweet. And look. You don't have to find stuff to tell me that's out of the ordinary. *You* are out of the ordinary.

HENRY. Really?

VIRGINIA. Really. I could listen to you talk about Personal Development Within Performance Review for hours.

Beat. They burst into laughter.

(*Pulling him, mock-seductive, towards her.*) In fact… it turns me on.

HENRY. I knew it.

(*Whispers.*) It's a *cross-faculty initiative*, you know.

VIRGINIA. Oh God. I *love* it when you talk dirty to me.

More laughter… and kissing. Lights down.

A video of Richard Feynman talking about quantum physics' incomprehensibility plays in the dark for a few seconds before it becomes clear that HENRY *is watching it…*

Lights up on: the university. TIM, HENRY*'s somewhat laddish mate, is pouring himself a coffee from a coffee machine.* HENRY *holds a remote control.*

TIM. You told Virginia about this? Are you mad?

HENRY (*pauses the video*). She trusts me, Tim. Correctly.

TIM. I know that. I just can't believe you told your wife – The World's Number-one Female Atheist Thinker – that you gave the time of day to a Christian.

HENRY. Less of the gender-specifics. She's just The World's Number-one Atheist Thinker, thank you very much, Professor Unreconstructed Fuckwit.

TIM. Shh. Never use my real name. Anyway –

HENRY (*raising the remote, pointing at screen where Feynman is still static*). Tim. I need to watch this.

TIM. Surely you've seen it before.

HENRY. Obviously. But it was made in 1964. If I'm going to show it to my students, now, I need to check it for… triggers.

TIM. Of course. At some point in this video Richard Feynman may have misgendered a proton. Is she attractive?

HENRY. Why do you want to know that?

TIM. Good question. Can't do anything with it any more. When I first set out on this career, it was the big bonus of being an academic. Some men join bands to get laid. I did a PhD in Computer Science.

HENRY. Because you wanted to have sex with spotty male geeks…

TIM. Stereotyping, I'll have you know, is a trigger for us… spotty male geeks. Anyway, by the time I was able actually to teach the – admittedly few – young women attending my classes, fraternising with them had become very much frowned upon.

HENRY (*nodding*). The History Man is history, I'm afraid.

TIM. It's so unfair.

HENRY. No it isn't.

TIM. Bear with me – I accept that attractive women get hit on a lot, unwantedly –

HENRY. Not a word.

TIM. …from powerful men and that's bad.

HENRY. Amazing. You've absorbed The New World, lesson one.

TIM. But what women don't realise is how difficult it is for men *not* to be attracted to attractive women. Or indeed all women. We're scientists…

HENRY. Well. You teach computing. So…

TIM. …and so we know that a positive charge will be attracted to a negative one. And to stop that happening is… well, it's impossible! Same with me. When I see certain… features, it's like, it *is*… magnetism.

HENRY. But somehow not the other way round.

TIM. That's the whole problem! If women *were* visually attracted to men, properly, if they understood the power of it, the fucking terror of it, of how enslaved we are; of having to go around with *these eyes*…

HENRY. Women *are* visually attracted to men, Tim. Just not fifty-year-old overweight men who dress like they're in a Status Quo tribute band.

TIM (*laughing*). How very dare you! You're fully aware I no longer play bass for *Quo-Incidence*. I still want to know what your quantum angel looks like though.

HENRY. Oh Christ. I thought you were with… what's-'er-name… Jameela? From the Faculty Library?

TIM. Over. In a trice.

HENRY. Really? You're amazing.

TIM. Thanks.

HENRY. No, I mean: at your age, still playing that game. I sort of admire it. Not so much the doing, more the constant moving on. Constantly having to end things. Isn't that difficult?

TIM. You get used to it after a while. I know you never could. How long were you with your first girlfriend? Sally?

HENRY. Annie.

TIM. Six years?

HENRY. Eight. The thing about you is you're such a great listener.

Beat.

I did try. To end it. Periodically. I'd work myself up to it and then… nothing seemed to be worth that much pain. I'd always end up thinking: I would rather be unhappy my whole life than have that conversation.

TIM. So what happened?

HENRY. How do you mean?

TIM. Well, you're with the wonderful, elegant Virginia. Who's not Sally.

HENRY. Oh! *Annie* left me. She'd been having an affair, it turned out, for two years.

TIM. Wow.

HENRY. Yes. When she told me, I was… fucking overjoyed.
A guilt-free break-up. A 'I'm not the bad guy' break-up.
I was so happy.

TIM. Did you manage to hide it?

HENRY. Quite well, I think.

TIM. And what about Virginia?

HENRY. Huh?

TIM. When are you going to get it up to tell *her* how unhappy
you are?

HENRY. I'm not. Everything's great. We're still making each
other laugh which…

TIM.…is the best you can hope for in marriage, I know. You often
tell me. So. Why are you mucking about with first-years…?

HENRY. Okay. Time to go and wind someone else up now.

TIM. Just tell me. What does she look like?

HENRY. See for yourself.

TIM *looks over. Spotlight comes up on* EDIE, *sitting in front
of the whiteboard, patiently waiting for the lecture to begin.*

TIM (*Martin Luther King impression, exiting*). Mine eyes have
seen the glory of the coming of the Lord!!! They have seen
him…

HENRY (*calling after him*). That's racism. You can be sacked
for that too, y'know!

TIM (*exiting*). Not if I do it like this!

(*Comedy Indian.*) Mine eyes have seen the glory of the
coming of Ganesh…

He smiles, shakes his head. Looks over at EDIE. *Flicks off
the video. Gathers himself, goes through into the lecture hall.*

HENRY. Hey! You're very early.

He begins wiping the whiteboard, arranging his papers.

EDIE. Sorry! Shall I wait out–

HENRY. No, no. It's fine.

EDIE. And sorry if – if I spoke out of turn the other day.

HENRY (*turning*). No! No, of course not. Please, you should feel free to ask anything. And besides, I worked something out. For you.

EDIE. Pardon?

HENRY. A calculation.

EDIE. You worked out a calculation for me?

HENRY. Yes.

He pours some water, slowly, into his glass. She comes over.

So. There are… how many H_2O molecules, would you say, in that half-glass of water?

EDIE. Um… I don't know. About… one-point-eight times ten to the power of twenty-four?

HENRY. Avogadro's number. Very good. Okay…

Writes it down.

How would you convert that amount of H_2O into the same amount of C_2H_5OH?

EDIE. C_2H_5… Ethanol…?

HENRY. I love a student who knows their organic chemistry. Yes, ethanol. Which is the best-known of *what* group of chemicals?

EDIE. The alcohols.

HENRY (*pouncing*). Alcohol! Exactly. Let's say a twelve-per-cent ethanol-alcohol content in the final substance, which I think is usual for… wine?

EDIE *smiles and frowns at the same time.*

EDIE. You've worked out an *equation* for the conversion of water to…?

HENRY (*enjoying it, deliberately matter of fact*). Yes. To convert H_2O to twelve-per-cent strength C_2H_5OH we have to add...?

EDIE (*beat*). C. Carbon.

HENRY. Yes. So where are we likely to find that?

EDIE. The air?

HENRY. Which contains carbon dioxide. So... it's then possible to set up this equation...

He finds a space on the whiteboard to write: '$3H_2O + 2CO_2 > C_2H_6P + 3O_2$'.

...which conserves the number of each type of atom. Let's assume this reaction is occuring at standard air pressure...

EDIE (*after a beat; she's joining in*). Well. We *know* the first time this... *reaction* occurred was in Cana. At a marriage.

HENRY. Right. Of course.

EDIE. And Cana was pretty near Nazareth which is three hundred feet above sea level.

HENRY. You've been there?

EDIE. I have.

HENRY. ...well, that won't materially change air pressure. So to calculate the total energy required to convert water and CO_2 into ethanol all we'd need to know is the energies holding together the underlying chemical bonds –

EDIE. – the bond enthalpies...

HENRY (*wrong-footed again by her knowledge*). – indeed, the bond enthalpies, we need a list of them and actually, 'here's one I prepared earlier'.

He clicks on a laptop.

EDIE. Sorry?

HENRY. 'Here's one I prepared...' – they used to say it on *Blue Pet*– probably not any more – never mind. There's the enthalpies...

The PowerPoint is on the whiteboard: a table of the bond enthalpies for each molecule concerned.

…if you add those up you get one thousand two hundred and fifty-five kilojoules…

Writes that down.

$$\sum \Delta H = 1255 kJmol^{-1}$$

…so now we can find the absolute amount of energy required to transform water to ethanol – although we need to know the original volume of water… what would the quantities have been at Cana?

EDIE. Quantities?

HENRY. How much water did Jesus make into wine? Exactly?

EDIE. I don't know. The Bible doesn't include his invoice for the catering.

HENRY (*laughing*). A joke. Excellent.

EDIE. Yes. Christians can make them, you know.

HENRY. Okay. Let's make it easy. Let's say it was a hundred litres of water. So the energy required to make that water a twelve-per-cent ethanol solution would be…

EDIE (*holds out her hand*). May I?

HENRY doesn't realise what she wants at first. Then, he does: the marker. He hands it over. EDIE starts writing, fast and furious. From here on, each equation is to be written at the same time as the speech below it is said.

Three molecules of water produce one molecule of ethanol –

$$\frac{x}{1 - 3x} = 12\%$$

– so to get twelve-per-cent strength you need to convert x where x is the amount of ethanol produced –

$$\Rightarrow x = \frac{0.12}{1 + 3 \times .12}$$

– so multiplying out and solving for x gives… point-twelve over one-point-three-six. Which is…

HENRY (*wrong-footed, he has to use an available calculator*). Er… hold on… er… nought-point-nought-eight-eight-two!

EDIE.…

$$E_r = \frac{(\sum \Delta H) \times \rho \times V \times}{M_-}$$

…so assuming the density of ethanol is roughly the same as water, V is one hundred litres which is nought-point-one cubic metres… the relative molecular mass of ethanol is… (*Tiny beat.*) forty-six, so putting all that in gives us…

HENRY (*presses buttons, trying to catch up: eventually*). – point-two-four-one. Gigajoules. Call it a quarter of a gigajoule.

She writes '0.241GJ' on the board and then puts the marker down. HENRY *looks on, very impressed.*

Amazing. Well done.

EDIE. So… it *can* happen.

HENRY. What?

EDIE. The miracle!

HENRY (*as if he's forgotten that's the point*).…Hm? Oh! Yes! As long as nought-point-two-five a quarter of a gigajoule of energy is brought somehow out of the air. By… Jesus.

EDIE. That's quite a lot.

HENRY. Yes. About seven-litres-of-petrol worth. Or seven hundred kettles boiling for two minutes.

She looks troubled for a second.

But I guess *that* is the miracle bit. And certainly using this as a starting point, you could, with a bit of mathematical jiggery-pokery, work out the – pretty low – *probability* of water indeed turning into wine.

Beat. Her face clears. She looks closely at the equation.

EDIE. It's beautiful. Beautiful.

HENRY. Well. I don't know about that. It's not E = MC squared. Or Dirac's…

Then, disconcertingly, she picks up the glass of water. She sips it.

EDIE. It tastes like wine.

HENRY. I beg your pardon?

EDIE. If you look at the equation – if you understand the equation – if you focus on the equation and forget everything else – then drink…

She drinks again.

…it's almost as if it does… taste like wine.

She holds out the glass to him. He smiles, uncertainly, wanting to say, 'This is a joke, right?' But her intensity says no.

He reaches for the glass.

Blackout.

Music: the screens again show a series of atomic fractals – but they should begin to be interspersed with something else – something religious – patterns from church windows that look similar.

Lights up on VIRGINIA *and* HENRY*'s living room. She is trying to pack an overfull suitcase.*

VIRGINIA. A book? A whole book?

HENRY. Is it that odd? The idea of me writing a book?

VIRGINIA. No! That's great! But… this?

HENRY. Well. *You* know how religion sells…

VIRGINIA. I *deconstruct* religion with logic and reason. I don't *bolster* it with them.

Her phone bleeps.

Fuck. The car's here already.

Looks at him.

Oh God, Henry, you really pick the best time to deliver big news!

HENRY. It's not that big news! You're taking it too seriously. The idea is… sort of a novelty book.

VIRGINIA. A novelty book is *How To Speak Klingon*. Not a book that shows you how, mathematically, a series of events that did not happen could in fact have happened.

HENRY. Ten grand. That's the advance HarperCollins would offer.

VIRGINIA. You've spoken to my publishers?

HENRY. Your agent.

Beat.

That's what Georgia guessed, anyway. Ballpark.

VIRGINIA *nods, silent.*

Sorry. I should have told you. But once I had the idea, I just thought I'd sound them out and –

Beat. She tries to shut her suitcase. Can't.

VIRGINIA. Urrrgh!

HENRY (*coming over*). You're taking too much stuff. You always pack too much stuff.

VIRGINIA. It's a lecture tour. There'll be lectures. And dinners. And daywear. I can't be fucked to work out an outfit for every day before I go. Too many choices.

Tries again to shut it – her phone rings – she speaks into it.

I'll be down in ten.

Beat.

Really? Okay, five.

Whilst she talks, HENRY *goes to sit on the suitcase.*

Traffic to the airport really bad, he says. Oh God oh God oh God…

HENRY *succeeds in zipping it up.*

Thanks.

Beat. He smiles a 'pleased to be of service' smile. She picks it up, moves towards the door. But can't resist…

What other – I'm going to use the word – it's not one I approve of – *miracles* are you and Ms Christian-Tits intending to work out the probability of?

HENRY. Do you approve of the words Christian-Tits?

VIRGINIA. Fuck yeah.

HENRY. Well… Red Sea parting.

VIRGINIA. Good one. Cos y'know… *that* happened. Definitely.

HENRY. Early estimates ten to the power of minus twenty-seven.

VIRGINIA. Right. And…?

HENRY. Manna from heaven. Water from a rock. Feeding of the five thousand. Resurrection of Lazar–

VIRGINIA. Ah, I thought so.

HENRY. What?

VIRGINIA. Just a cursory skip through the Old Testament. I bet Ms C-T –

HENRY. Christian-Tits.

VIRGINIA. With a hyphen – it's double-barrelled – I bet she'd prefer not to bother with those Jew ones at all. Just putting them in for the sake of balance. I bet she couldn't wait to get on to the proper stuff, the Jesus magic.

HENRY. V –

VIRGINIA. I mean, why stop there anyway? Why not work out the probability of Zeus being raised by a goat? Or us all being manifestations of the Thetan? Or the Second Coming happening in Missouri?

HENRY. Who believes that?

VIRGINIA. Mormons.

HENRY. Blimey. You know your stuff.

VIRGINIA. I'm serious, Henry. There's an agenda here.
A 'make Christianity zeitgeisty' agenda. Otherwise why not
include all other religions' miracles? They're *all* equally
improbable.

HENRY. We have discussed that, actually.

Beat.

For the next book.

VIRGINIA. Jesus wept.

HENRY. The probability of *that* having happened is quite high,
actually.

Beat; she doesn't laugh.

V. You haven't even *met* Edie.

VIRGINIA. I haven't. No. But I have a hunch that she doesn't
portend good things.

HENRY. I beg your pardon? The great rationalist – the great
materialist thinker – is proceeding over here on the basis of
a hunch? A bad feeling?

VIRGINIA. Oh fuck off, Henry. You know I read my horoscope
every day.

HENRY. Despite knowing, like we both do, that it's bollocks.
Typical Aries.

She does laugh at this.

But. You should. Meet her, I mean. I'm a teacher. Every day
I look out at a huge wasteland of uninterested adolescent
faces, just waiting for me to stop talking, so that they can go
and swipe right with each other.

VIRGINIA. Urrgh.

HENRY. And what you pray for...

(*Off her look.*) Okay, not pray for, what you *hope* for, but
never comes, is a student, who might be The One.

VIRGINIA. Pardon?

HENRY. Not in a romantic way. The One who makes you feel that teaching is worth it, because they've got ideas, they don't just sit there blank, they bring stuff to *you*, they make you think twice about what you're teaching, rather than not even thinking once, as you spout the same shit, year in, year out.

VIRGINIA (*softening*). Okay. I get that. You want a protégé. You want to be a mentor.

HENRY. Well. I guess.

VIRGINIA. But this way? Writing *this* book with her? About this?

HENRY. Look, V – as far as I'm concerned it wouldn't be a book about God, anyway. God is just a way in. To quantum physics.

VIRGINIA (*nodding*). Because both are beyond our understanding. As you said. But here's my issue, Henry. God is only beyond our understanding if you think He exists. Then – *of course* He's beyond us, in every way – beyond good and evil, beyond science – but if you don't, then there's *one* thing to understand, and it's very much *within* our understanding. Which is: we as a species are frightened. Of death. But also of life – of the dark, of what's round the corner, of pain – and what we'd like is to think that someone – that *Daddy*, basically – is going to make all that go away. If we're nice to Him.

HENRY. Virginia, I know. You're telling me something I know.

VIRGINIA. I know you know. But I think – if you're going to write this… book – I may just have to outline this again. Just to make sure.

HENRY. 'A close friend once said to me: but don't you *want* to believe in God? I said: yes. Desperately. That's why I *know* he doesn't exist.'

VIRGINIA (*taking aback*). You can quote the opening sentence of *The Belief System* by heart…?

HENRY. I'm a good husband. As I said.

VIRGINIA (*mollified, a little*). As I said. Sometimes.

HENRY. Listen. I understand that me writing a book like this is complicated for you. That it might be complicated for you *publicly*...

VIRGINIA. Henry, that isn't the reaso–

HENRY. Isn't it? At all?

She doesn't respond.

And if I can speak frankly... I've lived a long time in your shadow.

VIRGINIA *begins humming.*

Don't sing 'Wind Beneath My Wings'.

VIRGINIA. Sorry.

HENRY. I'm serious.

VIRGINIA. Sorry.

HENRY. And obviously that's been fine – more than fine – I'm so proud of you and your work. But I think I need to do this. I've only got one life and –

VIRGINIA. Do you?

HENRY. Sorry?

VIRGINIA. Well, you're the physicist. But I thought your whole shtick was infinite universes. Infinite universes, infinite lives.

HENRY (*beat*). Yeah. Well. I teach that. But I don't actually believe it.

VIRGINIA. Oh. Bit disappointing.

HENRY. Well, no, I believe it mathematically but... and anyway, every time you make a choice you collapse that infinite possibility...

VIRGINIA. Creating new infinite possibilities...

HENRY. Yes, but at the moment – my life – you know: it really doesn't feel full of *those*.

Her phone bleeps. She looks at it. She looks up.

VIRGINIA. Henry. This is important stuff. And we really need to talk about it. But –

HENRY. Can't keep the TED audience waiting.

VIRGINIA. TED will come calling for you soon.

HENRY. It'll be TED-X, I imagine. BTEC TED. My TED, in order to make himself feel big and important, calls himself Edward.

VIRGINIA. Henry. Write your book. Please. I can see how important it is to you. But: be careful. You know what – such a shit phrase – the *current climate* is like. Especially in academia.

HENRY. Christ, V, I'm not Tim. I'm not interested in –

VIRGINIA. I know, I know. But if you and a twenty-three-year-old student are going to be spending a lot of time together… Don't look at her the wrong way.

HENRY. V…

VIRGINIA (*very definite*). Don't write kisses after emails or texts. Don't call her love, sweetheart, or darling…

HENRY (*laughing*). Who am I, a plumber? From the 1970s?

VIRGINIA. And most of all… don't *touch* her. Not on the shoulder, to make a point; on the arm, to remind her of something; and never, never on the face – never place both hands on her cheeks, in what you think is a kindly, paternal way.

HENRY. Jesus.

VIRGINIA. I'm serious, Henry. I know your intentions will always be innocent. But we live in a world now where impact is more important than intent.

HENRY. Okay, okay. Yes. I get it. And you're right, of course. I promise.

Touches her hand.

It'll be a hands-free relationship.

VIRGINIA *smiles. She kisses him. Her phone bleeps again.*

She breaks the kiss.

VIRGINIA. Do you think there's a chance the book might be seen as a satire? On religion?

HENRY. Go catch your first-class flight to your big important lecture tour.

VIRGINIA *blows him a kiss, exits. Beat. Lights narrow on her, outside the door with her suitcase.*

The taxi driver appears to take her suitcase. Goes off. VIRGINIA *takes out her phone. Texts.*

The texts come up on the screen. Hers are to TIM.

VIRGINIA TEXT: 'T: May need a wing man.'

Text send sound. Lights up on TIM, *lounging on a sofa watching TV. Looks at phone.*

TIM TEXT: 'Always here 4 u.'

VIRGINIA TEXT: 'Bloody hell. Please don't write lol.'

TIM TEXT: 'I have limits.'

VIRGINIA TEXT: 'This Christian. Henry's co-writer. On his BOOK! Any info?'

TIM TEXT: 'She's hot.'

VIRGINIA *shakes her head.*

VIRGINIA TEXT: 'Creepy. What else? About – '

She pauses, then writes.

'Edie.'

TIM TEXT: A shrugging emoji.

VIRGINIA (*out loud*). A fucking emoji? Really?

VIRGINIA TEXT: 'What are we, Generation Zzzzzz?'

TIM TEXT: 'Nowt. Nada. Felch.'

New text: 'I mean Zilch. Ducking autocorrect.'

A door slam. A car engine starting.

Okay.

VIRGINIA TEXT: 'Can you find something out?'

Lights down. Lights up on: The lecture hall. HENRY is at the whiteboard. He writes: '$\Delta T = 1$ month later'.

Spread the light to show EDIE is seated there, with a laptop. On the whiteboard are many equations. He stands back and looks at the maths.

HENRY. ...this one isn't easy... then again, it probably wasn't for Jonah either...

Beat; he watches EDIE tapping away; she hasn't responded.

Shall we take a break?

EDIE (*looking up*). I think we've missed something.

HENRY. Really?

EDIE (*stands up, goes to whiteboard*). This is chemistry. When what we should be doing is physics. Quantum physics. I mean, don't get me wrong, Professor Brook – your water-to-wine calculation was brilliant.

HENRY. Oh, for Christ's sake, Edie. Time to call me Henry.

EDIE (*beat*). Well. Fine. Henry. Let's go back to when we first talked. About the miraculousness of quantum physics.

HENRY. I remember it well.

EDIE. I also mentioned the observer effect. I think we should give that more emphasis.

HENRY (*looking at the equation*). I can't see where it's applicable. There's no wave-function collapse.

EDIE. Isn't there? Quantum physics suggests that *everything* exists in a cloud of probability. *Everything*'s a wave function. Until the moment of observation. Us seeing the world is what makes it seeable.

HENRY (*beat*). Um... yeah?

EDIE. No but… so ignore the fact that that's quite a strong argument for the existence of God. Because if it's our minds that *make the world happen* – well – that would tie in neatly with the idea that He made us in his own image.

HENRY. Okay.

EDIE. Okay what?

HENRY. Okay, I'll ignore that.

EDIE (*laughing*). But what if – what if the miracles are happening all the time? Which they are…

She turns her laptop around. An animation is playing (there are many of these on YouTube) showing the double-slit experiment. It shows what she is saying.

…in the quantum universe – a single photon of light shot through two slits in a metal plate is travelling through both slits at the same time…

HENRY (*nodding*). A single photon is both travelling through both slits at the same time and not travelling through any and travelling through all other parts of the universe it could possibly exist in at the same time. I believe.

They watch as the electron splits infinitely onscreen.

EDIE. A miracle, right?

HENRY. Of sorts, yes.

EDIE. But the minute we try and observe that, or record it, it stops. It just becomes a single photon going through a single slit. When a torch is shone on the quantum world, it stops being… quantummy.

HENRY. Quantummy. I'm not sure Nils Bohr ever used that adjective. But yes: in the subatomic universe, everything exists in a cloud of infinite probability. What we can *observe* of that universe, what we can apprehend is, normally, just a single event within that cloud.

EDIE. Right. So let's say you *could* see a miracle – an electron being everywhere, OR – maybe – water turning blood-red at a marriage in Cana – that's a rip: between the macro world

and the quantum one. The observer effect hasn't *worked*.
We've been allowed to see under the quantum covers.

HENRY. It's an interesting i–

She has started walking to the whiteboard.

EDIE. Or perhaps… someone – something – has allowed us.
Because…

*She writes on the board. Equations to follow. They involve
infinity… and will include a Gd.*

…in the multiverse, everything that can happen *is*
happening. Somewhere. And *God*… has quantum eyes.
He can see infinity.

HENRY. I'm imagining a very big fly.

EDIE. Let's just think of Him as the Infinite Observer. Looking
at everything.

HENRY. Okay. So more like a security guard in a movie? With
loads of screens?

EDIE. Yes! So if on Screen X to the power of n, in Universe X
to the power of n, at one particular random instant, water is
turning into wine – God sees it, and He…

HENRY. Shuffles the screens…?

EDIE. Kind of. That energy is transferred. Across universes.
Through the eleven dimensions. Along the strings.

HENRY. Okay…

EDIE. Which means we should be able to create an equation
that charts the rip in spacetime that would allow for that to
be *observed* in *our* universe. For that *particular* wave-
collapse to be observed not just in Universe X to power of n,
but at Cana in 33AD. Something like…

She finishes writing.

$$E = \frac{i\hbar}{\sqrt{2}} \oint\!\!\!\oint \left[\frac{c^4}{4\pi K_\mu}(R - 2\Lambda + \mathcal{G}) + \mathcal{L}_m \right] \Gamma^\mu_{\nu\sigma} \frac{dx^\nu}{ds} \frac{dx^\sigma}{ds} d^4x \times \left(\frac{|\psi\rangle \otimes |\psi^*\rangle - |\psi^*\rangle \otimes |\psi\rangle}{\sqrt{|\det(g)|}} \right)$$

…this.

She looks up.

HENRY (*looking at whiteboard; shakes his head*). Wow.

He points to G.

What would you call that?

EDIE. The God Constant?

HENRY. The God Constant. I love it.

EDIE. Do you?

HENRY. Pardon?

EDIE. Well. You said it ironically.

HENRY. That's just because I'm a man. But seriously, Edie, it's amazing. You're amazing.

They are both close to the equation looking at it. He turns to her. He moves his hands as if to hug her... she smiles, receptive: she would be hugged... but then he doesn't.

It's supremely awkward: a stuck moment. And then, TIM enters.

TIM. Henry... you've got a lecture at four. Over in Hillier Hall.

HENRY (*checking watch*). Oh! Sorry!

TIM. The Sec asked me to find you – you weren't answering texts –

HENRY. I'm on my way!

Takes one last look at the equation.

Great work, Edie.

He exits. TIM *looks at the board. Then at* EDIE.

TIM. Looks good.

Beat.

The equation I mean.

EDIE (*shutting laptop, collecting her things*). I hope so. Sorry... Professor...?

TIM. Sabu. Tim. Pleased to meet you, Edie.

She nods, not engaging with the fact he knows her name.

So. This book. That you and Henry are writing… it'll have a Twitter page I imagine. Facebook, Instagram account?

EDIE. I suppose. Sorry, I wouldn't really know.

TIM. No. I guess not. Because *you* don't.

EDIE *frowns: what?*

Have a Facebook, or an Instagram account. No WhatsApp, no Snapchat, no TikTok, whatever the fuck that is.

He circles her; she doesn't respond.

Bit odd. For a member of… what are you? Generation Z?

EDIE. Have you been googling me, Professor Sabu?

TIM. Oh, so you've heard of it? The internet…

EDIE. Why?

TIM. Well, it's what people do… isn't it? Now. When someone new appears on the scene. In the old days, we'd have to actually talk to them, or even worse, just let them be, let them have their mystery, but now we google them, we *expect* to have… their information. So it's a bit suspect when there isn't any.

EDIE. Suspect?

TIM. Forgive me. I'm a computer scientist. And no digital footprint at all, suggests to the computer scientist part of me that that person has probably wiped it. For a reason.

EDIE *says nothing.*

Normally, because they have something in their past that doesn't fit with… who they are now.

EDIE. Or perhaps, that person just never bothered much with the internet. Because they didn't want to sully themselves.

TIM (*after a beat*). Henry's a lovely guy, isn't he?

EDIE. I think so.

TIM. But naive. Henry's unusual: in that he's kind of without subtext. He just says what he thinks. No agenda. And he doesn't therefore ever consider that other people might have one. But most people... do.

EDIE. What agenda do you think I have?

TIM. I don't know. I was wondering if you might tell me.

EDIE. Obviously that's something I'd love to do, professor, but I have another class to go to now.

TIM. No rush.

Beat.

Maybe over a drink, sometime?

EDIE (*leaving*). I'm really very busy right now. I have all my coursework and the book as well... maybe after the book comes out...

TIM. That's a while away, no? We can't have a proper chat sooner? After all, you owe me.

EDIE. I do?

TIM. In that I've chosen – for the moment – not to pass my suspicions on to my friend.

She pauses. Stares at him. Some coldness passes over her. Then, she nods.

EDIE. When the book comes out, I will.

TIM. Do I have your word? As a Christian?

EDIE. As all the things you assume me to be.

She leaves. TIM frowns, confused. He starts wiping the equations off the whiteboard, gets his phone out at the same time.

TIM. Hi...

A light finds VIRGINIA. She is about to go on to do her TED speech.

VIRGINIA. Hi.

TIM. Is now a good time?

VIRGINIA. Well, my talk is in five minutes.

TIM. I can call back.

VIRGINIA. No, that means it *is* a good time; it'll take my mind off it.

TIM. I can't believe you're still nervous about doing stuff like that. You'll be brilliant. You always are.

VIRGINIA. Thanks. So. How's it going?

TIM. Well, something is. Going on, I mean.

VIRGINIA. With Henry and Ed–

TIM. No, no. They're not…

He sees the word 'Entanglement' on the whiteboard. Wipes it off.

…at least I really don't think so. But with Edie. She's got a plan. Of some sort. But I don't know what it is.

VIRGINIA. Perhaps it just really is to spread the Good News about Jesus in a new science-y way.

TIM. She's too clever for that.

VIRGINIA. Career advancement?

TIM. She's too weird for that.

VIRGINIA. Well, you've been very helpful, Sherlock.

TIM. I haven't finished. She's an ongoing project.

VIRGINIA (*looking off*). Huh. I gotta go. Wish me luck.

TIM. Good luck. I'll continue to observe…

The sound of applause, off, as VIRGINIA *makes her way towards the lecture stage.*

The screens once again show a montage of fractals and religious images. And the applause off becomes applause in the room.

HENRY *enters, looking smarter, picks up from behind the lectern a glass of red wine. Writes on board: 'ΔT = a year later'.*

Lighting change. The whiteboard has become a flat, with a publicity photo of: GOD'S DICE: THE MATHEMATICS OF MIRACLES. *It's a book launch. Everyone has wine.*

HENRY *holds up the book.*

Forming a small audience is VIRGINIA, TIM *and* EDIE. *A sense of a bigger audience in sound.*

HENRY. Well. Ha. Um. For a physics lecturer whose only previous publication is one chapter on tachyons in *The New Scientist*, this is truly amazing. I really want to thank my publishers… the university for giving me the time and space to write… and, of course, Virginia. Because, hey that's what you do at these things, thank your wife, but also because… of her intellectual flexibility. There's been some silly things written in the press about, y'know, the great atheist thinker's husband writing a book about how miracles can really happen – and we all know that's not what the book is about – but I always knew she was too clever and nuanced-thinking to let any of that get to her. So, V – thanks for that, and for everything else, a thousand thanks.

A small round of applause directed towards VIRGINIA, *who demurs.*

And the other person I need to thank of course is my student Edie Eliot.

Focus on EDIE. *She looks shy.*

For saying something which gave me the idea in the first place, for back-up biblical knowledge and for really – can I swear? At a book launch?

TIM. Hey. It's *your* book launch.

HENRY. For really fucking helping with the maths.

Laughter. EDIE *demurs.*

Anyway, thanks again for coming, friends, publishers, colleagues, students – and: let's get drunk!

Applause. Cheers. He steps down from the podium. Goes over to group.

He kisses VIRGINIA. *Shakes hands with* TIM. *Raises a glass at* EDIE…

TIM. Great speech.

HENRY. No need to be sarcastic.

EDIE. I thought it was very good.

VIRGINIA. You're right, Edie. Of course.

She raises her glass.

Well done, Henry.

HENRY. Speaking as someone who's made a few speeches at book launches.

VIRGINIA. It's always a tough gig. Trying to sound all coy and self-deprecating when everyone's worshipping you.

HENRY. I'm not sure I've got to the worshipping stage yet.

TIM. Wait till you sell as many books as Virginia.

VIRGINIA. I'm not sure the next one's going to sell that many.

TIM. Bottom fallen out of the atheist market? You'll be pleased about that, won't you, Edie…?

EDIE. No. I mean… no, I wouldn't want anything… I wouldn't want you to sell fewer books, Mrs Brook.

TIM. Right. But you'd prefer it if more people believed in God. Which belief V's books somewhat pooh-pooh. On.

EDIE. Well. *I* believe in God. And I've read all her – your – books.

VIRGINIA (*taken aback*). You have?

EDIE. I respect – enormously – your opinions, Mrs Brook.

Beat.

TIM (*putting his arm around* VIRGINIA). I think this is the point, V, where you say 'And I respect – enormously – your opinions, Edie…'

VIRGINIA. Shut up, Tim.

HENRY (*taking* TIM*'s arm off*). Well, you could *maybe* reciprocate, V, just by saying how much you liked *God's Dice*. Because that is, in a sense, one of Edie's books.

TIM. Even though she didn't actually get a co-credit...

HENRY. Tim, I offered –

EDIE. And I declined. I didn't think it was important.

VIRGINIA (*beat*). Well. Yes. Of course. I liked *God's Dice* very much.

TIM. Any particular bit?

VIRGINIA. I'm going to say it again. Shut up, Tim.

HENRY. She's read it, Tim.

Noticeable silence from VIRGINIA.

EDIE (*smiling*). It's not a problem, Mrs Brook. I know you don't respect my belief. But I *do* like your books. Because they're written in a very... *Humble* – is that the word? – way. Some of the New Atheists... they're *so* convinced of their position, they come across a bit... arrogant. You know, they accuse people who believe in God of not listening to reason, but sometimes it feels like *they're* the ones blinded by faith, by absolute faith in their own rightness. But your books, Virginia –

VIRGINIA. Okay.

EDIE. No, I mean it. Really. *Your* writing...

VIRGINIA. Yes, thanks. I know what you're going to say. But really it's just a stylistic difference. Richard... dear old long-gone now The Hitch... they're bullish men – and they write like it. But the point is. They're *right*. They're completely right. So it's not arrogance. It's *frustration*. These are men possessed by truth, *frustrated* in the face of lies. Or rather, The One Big – the biggest – Lie.

Beat.

So, yes. I'm more demure than them – hey: I'm a lady – but I don't believe that God doesn't exist, I *know* He doesn't,

like I know that stone is hard. Sorry. But about the truth, I'm
no less…

(*Inverted commas.*) '…arrogant'.

Beat. She looks at EDIE. EDIE *returns her stare blankly.
Glances at* HENRY, *who is frowning.*

Sorry. I wasn't intending to get into this argument – not
tonight.

EDIE. It's okay. Please. I don't see it as an argument.

TIM. Right. It's just the kind of polite debate that happens
between scientists who don't believe in God, and those
who…

Gesturing HENRY.

…do.

HENRY (*laughing*). I *don't* believe in God.

TIM. But you don't *not* believe in God. Or at least your book
doesn't. Not. Fuck, there's a lot of double-negatives in this
discussion.

HENRY. The book believes, as physics is more and more
proving, that not-believing in the possibility of *anything* is
now foolhardy.

EDIE (*cutting through the banter with seriousness*). Kepler did.
Galileo did. Newton did.

Beat.

Believe, I mean. They believed.

TIM. Yeah, but they kind of *had* to? What with the other option
being burnt at the stake…?

EDIE. The book is called *God's Dice*, because Einstein said,
'God does not play dice.' Dirac said: 'God used beautiful
mathematics to create the world.' Schrödinger: 'The finest
masterpiece is the one made by God…'

VIRGINIA. Oh God.

Beat.

Fuck now *I've* used it. And I'm not even a great physicist. Look, they're using God as a metaphor, Edie. You know that. Einstein says God because of the poetry. It's more elegant to say God, than to say: The structure of the universe, the way that Nature is organised, doesn't play dice.

EDIE. Because even the greatest minds cannot think of a better word. Even Einstein, who invented a whole new understanding of the structure of the universe, cannot invent a more perfect expression for it than God. The whole universe packed into that tiny word: dense as a singularity.

HENRY. I read somewhere that forty-five per cent of British scientists are atheists.

EDIE. Which mean fifty-five per cent aren't.

TIM. Henry said you were good at maths!

VIRGINIA. Not being atheist doesn't make those scientists believers.

EDIE. No, but it means they believe in *something*. It means that like all the greatest physicists – Einstein, Dirac, Schrödinger, Planck, Pauli, Eddington – they are mystics.

VIRGINIA (*stumped; to* HENRY). Were they?

HENRY. Well. Yes. They all wrote philosophy about consciousness and being and stuff. Eddington even wrote *A Defence of Mysticism*.

VIRGINIA. Eddington. Wasn't he in *The Good Life*?

HENRY. Paul Eddington. Was Jerry. In *The Good Life*. Arthur Eddington – no relation – I think – wrote *The Internal Constitution of the Stars*.

VIRGINIA. Well. Interesting point, Edie.

EDIE. Thank you.

TIM. I can't believe you've caved so easily.

VIRGINIA. I haven't caved, you big twat. It's only in social media's 'ha you lost you got owned laughing crying emoji repeated twelve times' world that conceding a point is caving. In proper grown-up intellectual debate acknowledging your opponent has said something original and unexpected is a mark of intellectual security.

EDIE. I agree. We might be opposed intellectually, but can still find common ground.

VIRGINIA. Yes. And talking of common ground – you're right, Edie. I *am* different from all those New Atheist blokes. They think that to deny religion you have to hate it. I *don't*. I can see what's amazing about it. Religion has so much beauty and poetry and magic and… y'know: *showbiz* in it. And you kind of need that. Otherwise…

She holds up her copy of the book.

…you're just reducing God to a series of differential equations. Aren't you?

Beat. EDIE *looks very shocked. Her eyes moisten.*

Sorry – that sounded a bit too negative – about the book –

EDIE. No, no. It's okay. I take your point. I hadn't… I really hadn't thought of it that way. Excuse me.

Exits; beat.

VIRGINIA (*looking around*). Oh dear. Was I too harsh?

HENRY. She did help me enormously with the book, V…

VIRGINIA. Yes. I know. But… does that mean I'm supposed to agree with everything she says?

HENRY. Maybe… tonight. Yes.

VIRGINIA *nods. Lights down.*

Lights up on HENRY *and* VIRGINIA'*s living room. They come in, from the launch. In tense mode: they aren't quite looking at each other. They take their coats off, etc., without speaking to each other. Eventually:*

VIRGINIA. Are you coming to bed?

HENRY. Hmm?

VIRGINIA. Okay. I'll see you up there.

She moves to go: just as she's offstage…

HENRY (*it's been building*). I mean do you even know what a differential equation *is*?

VIRGINIA (*loud: from off*). Of course I fucking don't!

(*Comes back.*) I know what an *equation* is. I just added differential to sound flash.

HENRY. Well, it *worked*. Well done. You won the argument. Like you always do.

VIRGINIA. Oh Christ. I've said I'm sorry. Do I need to say it again? Sorry.

HENRY. It was my book launch, V. My bloody book launch. You couldn't put aside the argument-winning, just for one night?

VIRGINIA. Henry. Edie herself said it wasn't an argument. It seemed like she was loving it!

HENRY. Oh yeah. That's why she suddenly walked off, really upset!

VIRGINIA. That was the only time she seemed at all bothered! Before that, she's like: undentable. Nothing touches her. It's weird.

HENRY. And then just left! No idea where she went!

VIRGINIA. And that's okay, Henry. You're not responsible for her! She's your student, not your fucking daughter!

HENRY. No! She isn't! Not my daughter! Not my child! That's right! Because we don't *have* one of those!

VIRGINIA (*starting to leave*). Okay good. Let's wind back to that. Goodnight.

HENRY (*a burst of rage*). I mean… you haven't even fucking read the fucking book!

VIRGINIA (*taken aback*). Christ. Of course I have! You gave me the manuscript!

HENRY (*trying to calm down*). I know. But – but you never gave me any notes.

VIRGINIA. I said…

HENRY. Well done. Well done! You handed it back to me and said: well done. But you never said… 'This bit – I think that really works.' Or: 'I liked that chapter, but not that one.' Or: 'The cover's a nice colour but it could have done with a dash of pink.' *Something*. Something that tells me that…

VIRGINIA. What?

HENRY (*something pathetic about this, and he knows it: rage subsides*).…you've read it.

VIRGINIA. I… I *skim-read* it.

HENRY (*beat*). Skim… read.

Nods to himself.

Correct me if I'm wrong, but you're a speed-reader, aren't you? I mean, your default reading rate is like: the entire *Daily Telegraph* in under five minutes.

VIRGINIA. I don't read the bloody *Telegraph*!

HENRY. When I first saw you read the paper, the way you were turning the pages, I thought: this woman should be in the circus.

VIRGINIA. Be quite a shit act. Kids would definitely prefer the clowns.

HENRY. Anyway: so you read my book – even faster than usual…?

Beat; she nods.

Okay. Maybe we should move on.

VIRGINIA *goes to him, but he moves away. She shakes her head, leaves.* HENRY *on his own. Takes his phone out. Texts, to* EDIE.

HENRY TEXT: 'Where ARE you?'

Lights up on another part of the stage. A bar. TIM *is seated on a stool his own. He has a beer. There is a red wine as well in front of him. His phone is by the red-wine glass. Checks his watch, looks around.*

EDIE *enters.*

TIM (*standing up*). I thought perhaps you'd changed your mind.

EDIE (*sitting down*). I gave my word.

TIM (*sitting down*). In the beginning.

EDIE. What?

TIM. Was the word. Sorry. Shit attempt at a joke. I got you a red wine… hope that's okay?

EDIE (*looking down*). And a phone.

TIM *laughs politely, moves his phone closer to himself.*

That's a thing men do. At bars and restaurants. Put their phones in front of them. Women don't. Usually.

TIM. Hm. And why would that be?

EDIE. No idea.

TIM. Oh come now. I get the feeling *you* can break anything down to reveal its workings.

EDIE (*smiling*). Well… since if you *were* to get a text or a call, how long does it take to get your phone out of your pocket? Seconds – there must be another reason why men put it on the table.

TIM. Right, cos men do it even when they're out really late. When they wouldn't *want* to be contacted. Because it can only mean it's their wife asking where they are.

EDIE (*nodding*). Or someone's dead.

Reaction from TIM.

So. I'd say it's because the portable phone is the nearest thing men who aren't terrorists or Americans have to a gun.

She puts her hand in her pocket/bag.

So when men sit opposite each other at a restaurant and put their phones on the table, your pockets are your holsters, and in your head, someone has said: draw.

Takes her phone out in a cowboy way. TIM *laughs. She puts it down in front of her.*

TIM. Listen, I'm so glad you've come. I know I maybe applied a bit of… *leverage*… but you're fascinating. Really. I want to know you. I want to understand you.

EDIE. Why? Why do you need to pin me down?

TIM. Like a butterfly.

EDIE. Pardon?

TIM. 'You can pin and mount me, like a butterfly.'

Beat.

It's a Morrissey lyric.

EDIE. I don't know who that is.

TIM. Right. Of course… I just want to know your story. Why you're like you are.

EDIE. A Christian?

TIM. Well… yeah. That. It is confusing. In someone so clever.

EDIE. Because I believe in Jesus.

TIM. Yeah… but I mean –

EDIE (*calm throughout, never raises voice*). I know what you mean. What's the *real* reason? What do you want to hear? That I was brainwashed by evangelical parents? Had it whipped into me by sadistic nuns at convent school? Or that my dad abused me, systematically, between the ages of nine and twelve? And when he did, in order to disassociate from what was happening, I would see God? I would vacate my pained and traumatised body and wrap myself in the comforting arms of the Lamb?

TIM (*shocked*). I'm sorry.

EDIE. Don't be. I haven't said that's what happened. I just offered you a number of plausible – from your point of view – explanations. A point of view that assumes that religion, in a person of intelligence, must be a product of dysfunction.

TIM. That's weird.

EDIE. My story, you said. We're desperate for story, aren't we?
For cause and effect. For explanation. It doesn't need to be
true. It just needs to be satisfying.

TIM. I see. But I don't want a series of choices, Edie. I want to
know what's going on with you.

EDIE. That's the thing about things, professor. At heart:
unknowable.

TIM. Hmm. I know enough physics to take your point. I also
know enough physics to know that *you* are not a subatomic
particle. *They* might be unknowable, but people: they have
reasons – stories – discernable patterns – for why they are
how they are.

Beat. EDIE *nods*.

EDIE. What about you, professor? Where does the smug
certainty come from? The unshaken fundamentalist belief
that you know what's what? That the universe, for you, holds
no surprises? The banter and the knee-jerk negativity and the
deep protective armour of cynicism – what happened to *you*?
What trauma made *that* stick to your skin?

TIM (*beat; leans back; nods*). Well, Edie. Despite your
insistence on mystery, I feel like just in this short time I have
indeed got to know you a bit better.

EDIE. I'm glad. But this isn't really how you want to know me
anyway, is it? You want to know me in – what's the terrible
phrase…?

TIM. The biblical sense?

EDIE. The biblical sense.

TIM (*finishes beer*). Shall we just go back to mine?

*She looks at him. Then very deliberately, she puts her hand
on her phone and twists it towards* TIM.

EDIE. To pin and mount a butterfly, of course, you have to
catch it first.

Reaction from TIM. *Lights up on* VIRGINIA *and* HENRY,
as before.

VIRGINIA (*coming towards him*). Henry. If you're asking – basically – am I proud of you? For writing this book? The answer is: of *course* I am. I don't have to agree with everything your book says to be proud of you.

HENRY. Okay. Okay.

They kiss. Gingerly.

VIRGINIA. And I'm sorry about the row with Edie tonight. Again.

HENRY *nods*.

So. Are you coming to bed now?

HENRY (*opening a laptop*). Yes. Just need to check my emails…

VIRGINIA (*coming over, looking at his monitor*). Emails… or Amazon?

HENRY (*beat; embarrassedly*). You know me so well.

VIRGINIA. I know what being a published writer is like so well. What's it at?

HENRY. Fifty-eight on the Science and Maths chart!

VIRGINIA. That's fantastic!

HENRY. Three thousand and twelve on the overall… If only we'd got that quote from Brian Cox. He promised me!

VIRGINIA. I think that's still really good. For a new book.

HENRY (*nodding*). Obviously still well below *The Belief System*. Published four years ago.

VIRGINIA. Hey. Can we not turn into warring husband-and-wife writers?

Looks at screen again.

Promise me you and her are not going to fuck.

HENRY. What? Of course I'm not.

VIRGINIA. But you want to fuck her.

HENRY. I don't.

VIRGINIA. Oh piss off, Henry. She's twenty-three. She's menstruating. *I* bloody want to fuck her.

HENRY. V. I've been on my own – lots of times – with her, working on the book. Nothing's happened. What's different now?

VIRGINIA (*pointing to screen*). That.

HENRY *looks round*.

Success.

HENRY (*beat*). You're right. I may lose my marbles in the heady swim of being ninety-first on the non-fiction chart and decide to throw the best part of my life away.

VIRGINIA. So you promise…?

HENRY (*Scouts-honour salute*). I promise…

VIRGINIA. That was ironic.

HENRY. It'll have to do.

VIRGINIA (*smiling*). Okay.

Beat.

Am I really the best part of your life?

HENRY. That I do promise. Unironically.

She kisses him properly. He responds. Clothes begin to come off… Then, she notices something on the screen. Pulls back.

VIRGINIA. What's that?

HENRY. What?

VIRGINIA. That review.

HENRY. You were *reading*… while we were…? Do you often do that?

VIRGINIA. It's a five-star review.

He immediately stops complaining and looks round.

HENRY. Really? Oh good.

They peer in together at the screen.

VIRGINIA. 'On the pages of this book, man can hear at last the
voice of God speaking, as it was always meant to, through
science. Now, finally, we who have always known the truth,
have the PROOF – ' He's written proof in capitals.

HENRY. I can see that.

VIRGINIA. '*God's Dice: The Mathematics of Miracles* is
indeed a miracle. And the name Professor Henry Brook shall
be forever proclaimed, for the rest of time, in glory.'

They look to each other. Beat.

HENRY. Amen...?

Beat. They burst out laughing.

VIRGINIA (*through her laughter*). Oh Jesus. My husband's the
fucking Messiah.

HENRY. Do not take my name in vain, foolish woman, or
I shall have thee turned into a pillar of salt. And pepper. And
possibly piccalilli. A pillar of ALL the condiments.

VIRGINIA *gets up, still laughing. She makes to exit.*

VIRGINIA. Okay, that's slightly broken the mood.

HENRY. The sex mood?

VIRGINIA. Yes. But if you get upstairs quickly – you know,
maybe if you don't spend ages on miracle-ing up your home-
made bread to feed five thousand fans – we might be able to
re-establish it...

HENRY. They love my fluffy crumb.

VIRGINIA. I'm going to assume that's a euphemism.

She exits. HENRY *looks again at the screen, smiles, shakes
his head, gets up.*

*A Skype sound comes in. He frowns. Looks at screen. Looks
round, uncertain. Clicks on.*

Onscreen, it's EDIE.

EDIE. Hi! Sorry… is it too late?

HENRY (*looking round again*). Er… no, it's fine.

EDIE. Sorry, I was too excited. After the launch. I couldn't sleep. Did you read that Amazon review?

HENRY. Er… ChristTheKing97? Amazing.

EDIE. Isn't it?

HENRY. No, I mean amazingly… mad.

EDIE. Oh. It just made me excited. About what the book might be able to do for people.

HENRY. I'm more excited about what people might be able to do for the book. As in… buy it. In droves.

EDIE. Have you checked the Twitter page?

HENRY. We have a Twitter page?

EDIE. Of course we do. @GodsDice.

HENRY *clicks the mouse.* EDIE *shrinks into a box, behind her is a browser, he gets Twitter up on that.*

HENRY. Wow. Sixteen thousand. That's more than I was expecting.

EDIE. Refresh the page.

HENRY. Huh?

EDIE. Go on. Refresh it.

He does. Follow count now sixteen thousand and twelve.

HENRY. Wow!

EDIE. Every few seconds, there's ten more! At this rate, soon, you'll have hundreds of thousands.

HENRY. Not me. The book.

EDIE. You wrote the book, Henry.

HENRY *refreshes the page again. It goes to sixteen thousand and twenty-two.*

The light from his laptop intensifies, lighting his face in – yes – a godlike way.

HENRY. I did. I did. With a lot of help from you… And maybe you're right, maybe it will… do something for people. Make them… understand. Really understand.

VIRGINIA (*offstage*). Henry! You coming!?

HENRY *looks round. His face goes out of the light. Then he clicks back on the follower count. Up again.*

He moves his face back to the light.

HENRY. There we go. Another ten…

EDIE (*smiling*). Followers.

The light on his face intensifies.

HENRY (*beat; nods*). Followers. Of course.

Lights down. But the screen stays, with the image of the book, and the numbers spiralling. Plus numbers of it going up the book charts. Numbers turns to fractals and a ΔT saying 'Six months later'.

Lights up. VIRGINIA *is being interviewed at a literary/intellectual event, called 'Thinking Aloud'. Two chairs, with some kind of 'Thinking Aloud' banner. She holds her new book, which is called* Heaven Down Here.

VIRGINIA.…and so I suppose, yes, the basic point I'm making is that heaven *does* exist… here and now. Because if the early Christians could see the way we live now, here, in the affluent West, with its… supermarkets, and central heating, and life-saving medicines, and easy guiltless sex… it's paradise. What more could they want? For the people who invented the idea of heaven, this is heaven.

INTERLOCUTER. Thank you very much, Professor Brook. So… we've got ten minutes left. Do we have any questions? Yes – the gentlemen in the blue coat.

AUDIENCE MEMBER. Do you think that –

INTERLOCUTER. Just wait until the microphone gets to you.

AUDIENCE MEMBER. Oh sorry.

Microphone comes.

What I was going to say was... do you think that religion
will always be inevitable? In human societies? Or might we
eventually outgrow it?

VIRGINIA. Good question. I think when I was younger, we all
felt that society as a whole was progressing *away* from
religion, and that that would continue to be the natural arc
going forward – but of course we've now seen the opposite,
with the rise of fundamentalism and the re-emergence of
religion as a powerful cultural force, globally. I'd still hope
that as we move forward as a society then the *need*, the
psychological and cultural need, for religion, will fade, in
time. But recent history would tend to register me as an
optimist in that regard.

INTERLOCUTER. Okay.

*He looks out to audience. As he does so, lights up in a
different part of the stage. There is a bowl of fruit on a table,
a chair. HENRY enters. He takes his coat off, chucks it on
the chair. Takes his phone out.*

Any other questions?

HENRY (*into phone*). Hi. I know you'll still be onstage, but
I've arrived early so they've shown me into your – very nice
dressing room –

Picking up fruit.

– pomegranate: still never seen one of those in one of *my*
bowls – anyway, I'll just hang out here till you're finished.
But just didn't want you to get a shock when you open
the door.

INTERLOCUTER. Er... the man in the glasses.

HENRY. Hope it's going well, and that... you feel better about
everything now. See you in a few minutes, bye.

He clicks off, sits down. Takes a laptop out of his case, starts clicking.

INTERLOCUTER. Yes behind the – sorry – yes the guy standing up now. Thanks.

AUDIENCE MEMBER 2 (*loud*). What does your husband –

INTERLOCUTER. Can you wait for the mic please?

AUDIENCE MEMBER 2. – think of the book. Of all your books!

INTERLOCUTER. Hi, please can you wait – the mic will be there in a –

AUDIENCE MEMBER 2. She can hear me! *What does your husband think of your books!!*

This is loud enough for HENRY *to look round, frowning. A sense that he won't have been able to make it out, but would have heard something.*

INTERLOCUTER (*to* VIRGINIA). I'm so sorry, you don't have to…

Another AUDIENCE MEMBER *stands up, elsewhere.*

AUDIENCE MEMBER 2. Or to put it another way: what does a man to whom the glorious truth has been revealed – the glorious *scientific* truth – think of your LIES!!

VIRGINIA. My husband's book – the success of which I am very proud of on his behalf – is a conceit, not meant to be taken ser–

AUDIENCE MEMBER 3. Atheism has been *proved* wrong! By your husband! Why won't you acknowledge that?

VIRGINIA. Because I really don't think it has.

INTERLOCUTER. As I say, you don't have to respond to this kind of –

VIRGINIA. No it's okay.

Gathers herself.

You speak of proof… of the truth…

AUDIENCE MEMBER 2. Yes! And –

INTERLOCUTER. Please. Let the professor speak.

VIRGINIA....which is interesting, as we live of course now, in a post-truth world. Don't we? In fact, the way that *God's Dice* has become a small phenomenon is via the post-truth mechanism, the internet. If I understand correctly, the book proposes only a series of probabilities, some of them absurdly low, for various divine interventions. So none of them are proofs. But perhaps they are, because proof has become as pliable as probability. If nothing is true, *anything* can be true.

Looks out.

Can I ask you a question? Are you – any of you shouting at me – responsible for...

Gets out phone: scrolls.

...oh yes: @VirginiaBrookProf is a paedo hashtag-atheists-are-paedos hashtag-Hitler-was-an-atheist hashtag-Nazi-atheist-paedos?

Looks out.

No? Okay... what about @VirginiaBrookProf sucks Richard Dawkins' cock hashtag-atheists-go-dogging.

Laughter.

Yes, it's funny – except it isn't. Let me ask you another question –

Scrolling again.

...are any of you from...

Checks phone.

The Truth Gateway? A blog connected to this weird religious movement building around my husband's book...

Back to audience.

...on which on the 3rd of March this year, a series of emails were leaked in which I admitted to having plagiarised large sections of...

Holds it up.

…this book… from my students.

Silence.

Except I didn't. Plagiarise it obviously. But less obviously, write those emails. They aren't real.

Beat.

It's weird, isn't it? Because the internet *seems* to be all about having a multiplicity of voices. But actually, what's happening now is that the internet is being used to silence people. *Now*, if someone says something you disagree with, that you feel is a challenge to what you believe, you don't have to come up with an intellectual argument against them – just *lie* about them online. Soon… pfffff! Their voice disappears.

AUDIENCE MEMBER 2. The Word is in the Maths.

AUDIENCE MEMBERS 2 *and* 3. The Word is in the Maths.

AUDIENCE MEMBERS 1, 2 *and* 3. The Word is in the Maths.

They get louder each time. HENRY *realises something is up, rushes out of the room.*

VIRGINIA (*standing up*). Okay, I think we're done here.

AUDIENCE MEMBERS 1, 2 *and* 3. The Word is in the Maths. The Word is in the Maths. The Word is in the Maths.

INTERLOCUTER. Can we see if – can't we remove these people…?

AUDIENCE MEMBERS 1, 2 *and* 3 (*gradually louder*). The Word Is In The Maths. The Word Is In The Maths.

They keep going, chanting, louder and louder. VIRGINIA *gets up and walks towards the wings.*

HENRY *rushes on. She sees him. She shakes her head. He rushes over to hold her, protectively, but she keeps shaking her head.*

HENRY *still manages to wrap his arm round her. He looks out aggressively, raises his other hand.*

HENRY. Hey!

AUDIENCE MEMBERS (*a mess of overlapping, excited
    words*). The word is in the… Henry… that's Henry Brook…
    her husband… Henry Brook… actually HIM! Henry! Henry!
    Henry!

*HENRY's face changes from one of aggression to one of…
uncertainty. Of interest. Of liking this. Possibly.*

But before that completely resolves…

*Blackout. The screens go crazy: in the fractals and church
windows now, there are cult images, occult ones, etc., etc.
Fractals merge with butterfly wings, fast-cut images from
Twitter, Facebook, Snapchat, Satanic images of VIRGINIA,
terrible tweets, 'FUCK HER', 'RAPE HER', with others,
'GOD IS SCIENCE', 'GOD SPEAKS WITH EQUATIONS',
'THE WORD IS IN THE MATHS'.*

*It ends with a brand image of 'The God Constant': a smiling
but terrifying picture of EDIE, holding the book, with a
congregation behind her.*

ACT TWO

*The guitar part from 'Do Anything You Wanna Do', again.
Lights up on a quote by Carl Sagan from* The Pale Blue Dot.

*Mix in sounds of the sea, under the guitar part. As these
increase, lights up more to reveal the Sagan quote is in fact
a poster, up on the wall of a shabby-chic café in Cornwall.
It's called The Butterfly. Music plays in the background. The
whiteboard is now a blackboard, showing food with prices.*

HENRY *is seated at a table. He is more smartly dressed than
before: more expensive clothes. But looks exhausted. An
insouciant waiter –* BILLY *– comes by.*

HENRY. I'm just… waiting for someone.

BILLY. Oh, okay. We're closing soon, so if you want something
you might want to order… like now.

HENRY. Oh. Okay. A… flat white please.

BILLY. Okay, whatever.

BILLY *goes. Few seconds later,* EDIE *enters. She looks
somehow older, more confident. She smiles and runs over.*

EDIE. Hey! How *are* you!

*She makes to kiss him on the cheek. He moves away. He says
the next words to cover the awkwardness.*

HENRY. I'm… I'm never sure about where the stress should be.

EDIE. Sorry? You're stressed?

HENRY. Well… yes. Actually. But I mean: on how are you?
I think I normally say how are *you*? But you said: how
are you?

EDIE. I think you're overthinking it.

HENRY. I thought religious people believed there was meaning
in everything.

EDIE (*smiling*). Answer the question.

HENRY. What question? Not the one about 'If I believe in…' what was it? 'Quantum entanglement or something shouldn't I believe in God?'

EDIE. No, you answered that one. In a roundabout way. No. How are you? That question.

HENRY. I'm okay.

EDIE. You're looking…

HENRY. Stressed?

EDIE. Smart.

HENRY. Yes, well. One advantage of being a university lecturer who's written a successful book is not having to dress like an university lecturer any more.

EDIE. And Virginia? How's she?

HENRY. Well. She's kind of why I'm here… why I've driven two bloody hours to –

BILLY *reappears*.

BILLY. So… would you like some… hey! Edie!

EDIE. Billy, hi! How *are* you?

HENRY. You see, not… how are *you*?

BILLY (*makes a 'Who is this twat?' face; then*). I'm good. I'm coming tonight. To the service.

EDIE. Great!

(*Slyly*.) Do you know who this is, by the way?

BILLY (*looks at* HENRY). No, sorry. Should I?

HENRY. Edie –

EDIE. It's Professor Henry Brook.

BILLY *stares at him. Then back at* EDIE, *like… 'No!' She nods. Beat.*

In one swift motion, BILLY *falls to his knees.*

HENRY. Oh for fuck's sake.

BILLY. Forgive me!

HENRY. What the fuck for?

BILLY. I was rude to you earlier!

HENRY. Well, yes, you were a bit…

BILLY. Then I made a 'Who is this wanker?' face!

HENRY. Did you?

BILLY. FORGIVE ME!!

HENRY. Alright, I forgive you! Jesus!

EDIE. Billy. Let's not forget. He's only a *man*.

BILLY (*getting up*). Thank you, Professor. Thank you. Is there anything I can do? Anything?

HENRY (*beat*)….A flat white? No sugar?

BILLY….Okay!

He exits, quickly.

HENRY. Bloody hell. Are you all like that?

EDIE. Well. I'm not. Or haven't you noticed? Billy's new to us. And a little… eager. You'll see when you meet the others, there's lots of different types of –

HENRY. Meet the others?

EDIE. Yes.

Beat.

Don't tell me you've come all this way and you're not even going to come and see what's happening in your own movement.

HENRY. *It's not my…* is that what you call it? Movement?

EDIE. Yes.

HENRY. Not cult.

EDIE. Not cult.

HENRY. It's an unfortunate word, cult. So easy to mishear.

EDIE. Our official title is 'The God Constant'.

HENRY. Yes. I know. I was thinking of suing for copyright.

EDIE. I believe the phrase was my idea in the first place.

HENRY (*waving it away*). Anyway, no. I'm not coming to meet the other members of…

EDIE. TGC for short.

HENRY. I've come to ask you to stop it.

EDIE *frowns*.

Virginia is in danger of having a breakdown.

EDIE. Because of…?

HENRY. Because of your fucking *cult*. Putting the frighteners on her. Hate mail. Trolling. Barracking at her events.

EDIE. I assure you the people behind all that were not representative of TGC.

HENRY. Well, they were carrying copies of my book!

EDIE. I am sorry, Henry. Early on, when the movement started, there were some that felt that for too long Christianity had been the one religion that – I don't know – was always fair game. That we had lain down and taken it all, all the *sneering and the jokes and the blasphemy…*

Slightly loses herself: recovers.

…while other religions: well; their response had been more *muscular.*

HENRY. Muscular. Beautifully put.

EDIE. Even the Pope has said, if you insult someone I love, expect a punch.

HENRY. I believe someone else said, turn the other cheek.

EDIE. Yes. He also said 'I come not with peace but with a sword.'

HENRY. Always was a contradictory bastard.

EDIE. Anyway, there were people who felt that when The Book came out, that now we Christians finally had proof. And with proof came... a certain *militancy*. For which I apologise, and assure you that we in The God Constant do not condone it.

HENRY. Clearly, you're high up in The God Constant. You sound like their PR spokesperson.

EDIE. It isn't just your wife, of course. Richard Dawkins –

HENRY. I know others have got a piece of TGC's militant tendency. But *she's* getting particularly nasty treatment. *Because* she's my wife.

EDIE. But why would Virginia blame you? She must know that none of it is your fault.

HENRY. When did I say she blamed me?

EDIE. She doesn't?

HENRY. *Of course she fucking does!*

Beat.

I wrote the book. So it's very very hard for her not to blame me. She's only human.

BILLY *approaches with a flat white. He lays it down, almost ceremoniously.* HENRY *nods, wearily.* BILLY *exits, backing away, as if from a Royal;* HENRY *watches him incredulously.*

Unlike me of course.

Beat, shaking his head.

Hashtag-not-a-cult.

EDIE. Well, we'd be the first religious cult without a charismatic *man* at the helm. It's normally someone with at least a beard...

HENRY. A charismatic woman, though. Which you've very much become.

EDIE (*almost to herself*). Oh yes there's always women around, organising, servicing, but the worship instinct? That seems to need a Y chromosome. God the Father, God the Son…

HENRY. Wow. You sound like Virginia.

EDIE. We're not so dissimilar. We both think the key is to *understand*. Do *you* want us to stop?

HENRY. Pardon? I just said –

EDIE. You're telling me what's best for your wife. But what do *you* want?

HENRY. I… yes. *Of course* I want you to stop. I want to end it.

EDIE. You don't seem very sure about that.

Beat. They stare at each other. She sighs.

You know when someone is in love with someone else, and then they find out that that love is unrequited – they say, don't they, 'Oh: I can't believe you don't feel the same way.' Or something.

HENRY. Yes…?

EDIE. Can I say that to you?

HENRY (*taken aback*). Sorry? About… us?

EDIE (*beat*). No. Sorry. I meant – about the book. About *God's Dice*. I guess we spent so much time together – working together – that I can't believe… that you don't feel the same way.

HENRY. Oh. I see. About God.

EDIE. Yes. About God.

Beat.

And this is the part where the unrequited person says… 'Not even a little bit?'

Beat.

It didn't shift your certainties at all? All those equations? All that proof?

HENRY. Those equations aren't proof, Edie. You know they aren't. They can't shift any certainties.

EDIE. Perhaps. What they can do, though, is measure *un*certainty. And as Heisenberg can tell you, that is the nearest we can get, now, to the truth.

HENRY (*beat*). You're very clever, Edie. You always were. What about you? What about your studies? What about the physicist you could have been?

EDIE. I study here now. I'm being that physicist, here.

BILLY *re-enters with a copy of* God's Dice. *He holds it reverently. He approaches the table.*

BILLY. Sir...

HENRY. Please don't call me sir. I prefer Lord. Or just Holy One, Blessed Be He.

BILLY *unsure...*

Henry. Henry is fine.

BILLY. Heh. Yeah. Um... can you sign The Book?... Henry.

HENRY *nods. Opens the book. Takes a pen out.*

HENRY. Just the regular signing, with...

(*Of pen.*) ...this, or would you prefer my name emanating from the page in blood?

BILLY *frowns again.*

I'll still put 'To Billy, best wishes...'

EDIE. Just sign The Book, Henry.

HENRY *signs.* BILLY *takes the book, looks at the flyleaf in awe.*

BILLY. Thanks... Professor Brook.

Exits.

HENRY. I have a horrible feeling that when you and he are saying the words The Book, in your minds, you're capitalising the T and B. Tell me you're not.

She just smiles at him; he puts his coat on.

So. You won't wind it up. The movement.

She doesn't respond.

Because so far I've not made a public statement, disowning your activities. But I will. I will, Edie.

EDIE. Henry. Just come and see. We're not what you think. We have classes: physics, maths, astronomy. We debate. We experiment. It's intellectually rigorous. We've found a new path between science, religion and philosophy. The Book – it's led to a whole new way of thinking about God. We're making religion tenable, credible – a belief system that throws off the ludicrous Creationist evangelicals to create something new.

HENRY. It's a big rebrand.

EDIE (*laughing*). Yes.

Holds out her hand.

And also… *I'd* like you to come. I'd like you to see… our Church.

He looks at her. Some sense of exhaustion in him. He doesn't take her hand.

Lights down. On the screen: YouTube. VIRGINIA's TED Talk, the one she went to do in Act One. She looks great, confident.

VIRGINIA (*off*). Anything that we want so much we will call into being. Anything so deeply desired as this – a fantasy superhero Dad who chases off death – we will project him into the skies. We will make him real.

Lights up. HENRY and VIRGINIA's living room. VIRGINIA is watching herself on a laptop. She looks considerably not as good as onscreen.

She has a glass of wine, and a bottle. There is another empty bottle. She is wearing a dressing gown.

Her text 'ting!' goes. She stops the film. She looks at her phone. We don't see HENRY's text. But she types.

VIRGINIA TEXT: 'No problem darling. I won't wait up.'

She sits and looks at the text for a while. No response.

HENRY TEXT: 'Thanks. I love you.'

VIRGINIA TEXT: 'And I you xxxx'

She clicks off the phone. Gets up. Seems to making for bed. Then, a doorbell buzz.

She frowns. Goes over to it.

Silence.

Hello? Look if it's… someone from… that cult – if you've somehow found where we live – I'll call the –

TIM. Sorry, Virginia. It's me. Tim.

VIRGINIA (*does her belt up, opening the door*). Tim?

TIM. Hi. Look, it's obviously too late – I'll –

VIRGINIA. No, no. Come in.

She buzzes. Sounds of distant door opening. She makes a cursory check on herself in a hallway mirror.

TIM comes in. They kiss on the cheek.

Hi…!!

TIM (*seeing that she is not properly dressed*). It's really not too late?

VIRGINIA. It's not *late*… I've just started to go to bed early. But happy to put it off for you. Would you like a drink?

TIM. Are you sure?

VIRGINIA. If I want to offer you a drink?

She pours him a drink; they sit.

TIM. No are you *sure* you don't want to go to bed. I was only coming by to –

VIRGINIA. To what?

Beat.

Check on me?

TIM. Kind of.

VIRGINIA. Is it out in the world then? That I'm having a breakdown?

TIM. No, not at all. Just – a couple of things Henry said…

VIRGINIA (*nodding*). 'She's not sleeping', 'she's bursting into tears'. 'She's…

Downs her glass.

…drinking much more than normal.' That kind of thing?

TIM. I know you've been under a lot of pressure. Since Henry's book came out.

VIRGINIA. Tell me about it.

TIM. So I just thought maybe you could do with someone to talk to. Who wasn't… Henry.

VIRGINIA (*beat; frowning*). Did you get back early then? From the conference?

TIM. Sorry?

VIRGINIA. The one-day conference. In Bristol. That you and Henry were going – okay, he's having an affair now, as well. Brilliant.

Drinks more wine.

TIM. No!

VIRGINIA. I don't blame him. It must be a nightmare coming home every night to a sleepless, weepy alcoholic.

TIM. Look, whatever Henry told you… I'm *sure* he's not having an affair.

VIRGINIA (*hard*). Is there a conference on lattice gauge theory? In Bristol? Or anywhere else.

Beat.

Tim. I need you to be honest with me.

TIM (*deep sigh*). Not that I know of. I don't actually know what lattice gauge theory is.

VIRGINIA. You should have lied.

Takes a deep drink.

TIM. He's not being unfaithful, Virginia. Not in that way.
I really don't think so. And… I wouldn't know about *any*
conferences now anyway.

VIRGINIA. What? You love a conference – all those hot young
female lecturers, all looking up to the older still-handsome-
in-a-kind-of-shlubby-way computer scientists…?

TIM. I – oh God, I may as well play it to you.

He takes out his phone. She frowns. Lights down.

Lights up on another part of stage. HENRY *and* EDIE *enter
a bare room, with an old chair and desk, with a laptop on it.
A smock, with a cool TGC design on it, hangs somewhere.*

HENRY. This is it…? The Great Cathedral of the God
Constant?

EDIE. The chapel is upstairs. This is where I get ready.

HENRY. To meet your flock.

EDIE. If you like.

HENRY. It's a… service? You pray?

EDIE. Yes. But only in a way that makes sense within the laws
of physics.

HENRY. Okay now you've lost me.

EDIE. You need to see it.

HENRY. When does the service start?

EDIE. Midnight. Well, just before.

HENRY. Midnight?

EDIE. We often meet then. It's the best time to plug into our
global network.

(*Off his frown.*) Oh yes. There's TGCs now in America, in
Germany, one just forming in Beijing.

She clicks on the laptop. On the screen/whiteboard, comes up various screens, images of The God Constant website in different languages, different global places.

HENRY. Well. That *is* amazing…

EDIE. Also: there's an extra… spiritual energy generated by it being midnight.

HENRY. Right. Bit Aleister Crowley…

She looks confused.

I always forget how young you are. He wrote spooky books about the occult.

EDIE (*smiling*). Spooky action…

HENRY. Maybe. Perhaps not at enough of a distance though.

EDIE. I'd love you to stay. We're planning a big event tonight.

HENRY. Something… miraculous?

EDIE. Possibly.

HENRY. I was being ironic.

EDIE. I know.

HENRY. You *have* changed… Well. I can't stay till then anyway. I told Virginia I was going to be late back. But not that late.

Beat.

I didn't in fact tell her I was coming here at all.

EDIE. You didn't?

HENRY. No, I told her… something else.

EDIE. If you told her, you'll be back late, be back late. Drive back after our service. Exeter's only a couple of hours away.

HENRY. No… Edie.

(*Of the websites.*) It's… I dunno… it's flattering all this. That it all came from the book. But it's also mental. And I came here not to join in, but to ask you to stop.

EDIE. We can't.

HENRY (*laughing*). What, because of destiny? Because it's preordained? Because of God's plan?

EDIE. 'But do not overlook this one fact, beloved, that with the Lord one day is as a thousand years, and that thousand years as one day.'

HENRY. Pardon?

EDIE. It's the Bible. Peter 3:8. But Einstein agrees: time exists not as a continuum but in a block. A four-dimensional block of eternal spacetime.

HENRY. All you're proving, Edie, all we ever proved, is that science can be repurposed as religion. Or to be more exact, re*phrased* as religion.

EDIE. Relativity means that our future, to another observer, may have already happened. Is that not a plan? Not destiny?

HENRY. Great. Relativity means everything is predetermined. Quantum mechanics says everything is chance. How the fuck is one supposed to make sense of all that?

EDIE. Sense isn't what you need. Belief is.

She goes to the whiteboard. She starts to write an equation. Lights down.

Lights up on TIM *and* VIRGINIA. *He holds up his phone (or it's on the table, prominently).*

EDIE'S VOICE ON PHONE. To pin and mount a butterfly, of course, you have to catch it first.

He clicks it off. VIRGINIA *looks shocked.*

VIRGINIA. That was… you and Edie?

TIM (*nodding*). I met her for a drink. After the book launch. Nothing… happened. Well. Except that. Her recording our conversation on her phone.

VIRGINIA (*beat; stares at him*). What did the word 'leverage' mean there…?

TIM. It means I had some suspicions about her; that I chose not to communicate to Henry…

VIRGINIA. You were saying, then, that you'd done her a favour. And that therefore… she owed you.

He nods, ashamed.

Okay. Well. Even for you I'm surprised. You really shouldn't have done that, Tim.

TIM (*nodding*). You're completely right.

VIRGINIA. I'm glad you agree, for once, that your behaviour was reprehensible and wrong. Or am I picking up… another reason for that agreement?

TIM (*still nodding*). Yesterday, she emailed that recording to the entire Board. All the staff have probably heard it by now.

VIRGINIA. Fuck.

TIM. I've been sacked, Virginia. And I'll never get another job in academia. So: no more conferences for me, I'm afraid.

VIRGINIA. Fuck.

Beat.

Even though she's left the university now? Can't you claim this was just you chatting up an independent young woman…

TIM (*shakes head*). She was still a student when this happened. And anyway, details don't matter. You know that. Not in the great redress. The great corrective.

VIRGINIA. No. Well. Sometimes they do, and sometimes they don't. And in this case, I'd agree: they don't.

TIM. Okay. But it was *your* idea. In the first place.

VIRGINIA. What was?

TIM. That I should investigate her. That I should find out more about her.

VIRGINIA (*stares at him*). So it's my fault? That you tried to leverage her into sex…?

TIM. Well…

VIRGINIA. Fuck me. I'm a prize-winning academic, I've written five books about the oldest patriarchal myth, and still I have no idea how men simultaneously manage to hold all the power and none of the responsibility. Do you not *listen* to Spider-Man?

TIM *laughs, and shrugs.*

And anyway: you *didn't* find out anything about her.

TIM. I found out a number of things, actually. Including that she was abused by sadistic nuns. And her dad.

VIRGINIA (*taken aback*). She was –

TIM. I just don't know if any of them were true.

VIRGINIA (*after a beat*). Why would she say stuff like that if it wasn't true?

TIM. She seems to take Heisenberg very seriously. For her it's a matter of principle.

VIRGINIA. Yeah, very good, Mr Wordplay. But the uncertainty principle states only that the more accurately you can measure the position of a particle, the less accurately you can measure its momentum.

TIM. Blimey. And Henry thinks you never listen to him.

VIRGINIA. It's got nothing to do with the real world. With humans, with personality.

TIM. Yes. But in all seriousness, I think Edie believes in the quantum world like she believes in God. Fervently.

VIRGINIA. Or maybe she was just trying to fuck with you. Because you were trying to fuck her.

TIM. Maybe. But now, I *have* found something out about her.

He holds up his phone.

She is powerful. She is dangerous.

VIRGINIA. Yes. Well. *That* I agree with. Which is why I'm glad she's fucked off to Cornwall. At least Henry isn't in *her* orbit any more.

Beat. TIM *looks troubled.*

TIM. Sorry, I didn't mean to come here with all my problems. I'm here because I'm your friend. Your oldest friend, I believe.

VIRGINIA. Longer than I like to think of…

TIM. Yes. In my darkest moments… like, say, now… I often comfort myself thinking of the lovely life we might've had together if only you'd said yes that one time I asked you out. Why didn't you?

VIRGINIA. You asked if I wanted to go and see *Beaches*. *Beaches*! Surely you didn't really want to see *Beaches*?

TIM. No. I thought – I thought it was the sort of movie a… lady would like…

They burst into laughter.

VIRGINIA. A fine lady!

TIM. Why did you say no?

VIRGINIA. *I didn't want to see fucking* Beaches*!* If you'd suggested *RoboCop*, we might be celebrating our thirtieth wedding anniversary by now!

TIM (*beat*). Really?

VIRGINIA. What really?

TIM. Was that all it was?

VIRGINIA. What are we talking about now?

TIM. Do you really think we might have – if things had been different…

VIRGINIA. Oh Jesus. Tim. Come on.

TIM. V – I've always –

VIRGINIA. Tim. Everyone in the university – everyone in *academia* – knows that you spend half your time lusting after the female students and the other half complaining how it's not acceptable any more for middle-aged academics to lust after the female students.

TIM. Yes. Okay. But maybe I'm like that because… I never found anyone, Virginia.

VIRGINIA. Er… I believe you found many, many –

TIM. Who could match up with you.

VIRGINIA *bursts out laughing.*

Don't laugh at me.

She carries on.

Okay, sounding that self-pitying normally stops people laughing.

VIRGINIA. Sorry. You're right.

Beat. Tries to control herself. But then the laughter bursts out again.

TIM. Virginia. I'm trying to tell you I'm in love with you. I've always been in love with you.

She howls with laughter. Finally she calms down. Beat.

VIRGINIA (*with greater sympathy*). Timothy. Here's the thing. You're not in love with me. When what you're in love with – if you're in love with anything at all – is a memory of what I was like when I was twenty. Or more likely: when *you* were twenty. That's what you're in love with, Tim. 1987. Mullets. The Thompson Twins. And most importantly, your long long distance at that point from death. You know what you're in love with, Tim? Time. A sense that your life then had so much *time*. So much yet to come.

TIM. You see, that's why I love you.

VIRGINIA *frowns.*

Because you're always right.

Beat.

Are you not even flattered?

VIRGINIA. No. You're too much of a twat.

Beat.

And also, you're feeling sorry for yourself, and when men like you feel sorry for yourself you like to project your self-pity into some grand lost passion.

TIM. Well, this has gone well.

VIRGINIA. And more importantly… you said when you came in you thought I might want to talk to someone who wasn't Henry. So… You knew Henry wouldn't be here. Didn't you? When you came over. Which means that even though you don't know what lattice gauge theory is, you know where my husband actually is right now. Don't you?

Lights up on HENRY *and* EDIE, *as before.* EDIE *is still writing the equation, it is now very long.*

EDIE.…So clearly the second derivative with respect to the underlying parameter is the normal metric expansion of the Christoffel connection times the geodesic differential…

HENRY. Stop, Edie.

EDIE.…which clearly reduces to two dee-mu phi at X-nought eta alpha-beta dee x-nought mu by dee lambda…

HENRY. Please, Edie. Stop. If you're hoping to make me *believe* with this… I need something else. Something that isn't just maths.

EDIE (*still writing*). What might that be?

HENRY. I don't know, Edie. I don't know.

EDIE (*still writing*). There is nothing that is not-maths. Even the *concept* of nothing is maths.

HENRY. I know… yes – but please. Stop. None of this will make me believe!

EDIE (*still writing*). I *know* you don't know if you believe in Go–

HENRY. NO! Physics! I mean, of course, I believe the equations – I know the numbers work – but all the weirdness of quantum mechanics, relativity – time travels slower as you go faster – really? Does it? I've never noticed it happening in my Mazda, not even speeding on the M5!

An electron is a wave *and* a particle? Really? Show me it! Show me it washing around like a pebble in a tsunami! Sorry, sorry: a pebble that is *also* a tsunami! Yes, Schrödinger's Cat, mathematically, is alive and dead at the same time, except WE ALL KNOW IT ISN'T. WE ALL KNOW IT'S ALIVE OR IT'S FUCKING DEAD.

EDIE just continues, impassively, to write.

Stop, Edie. Stop. Please…

And he reaches out and grabs her wrist. Music: the full version of the slow melancholic acoustic version of 'Do Anything You Wanna Do'. Lighting change.

She turns to look at him. His hand stays on her wrist. His other hand comes up to her cheek. Their eyes meet. It's a tableau: in an ideal world, it would revolve.

The laptops onstage, everywhere light up, with atoms, dancing. With entangled particles.

Hold that. We see his sadness and pain and desire which IS desire for her but also for what she represents: for transcendence, a yearning to be at the same place of belief and wonder…

Lights come up on TIM *and* VIRGINIA. *Music continues underneath.*

TIM. I'll take you to him. To them both.

She frowns, puts her drink down. Gets up. She wobbles as if she might fall. TIM *gives her a hand.*

VIRGINIA. Maybe I shouldn't go.

EDIE. *Now* do you believe?

Blackout.

Flashing. Shapes and fractals. Shapes and fractals, and religious imagery. Music builds.

Lights up on: The chapel of The God Constant. It's a white space, with a central altar surrounded by video screens. Various members of The God Constant sit in front of it, but the sense should be that the audience in the theatre provide the wider congregation (place extras in audience to create that sense).

Slowly, robed in white, EDIE *takes the altar. She holds a remote control/PowerPoint controller. She faces the congregation. Beat.*

It's tempting, you know, to use antiquated language when you're up here. For some reason, I feel an urge to say not 'Hello' to you, tonight, or 'Good evening' but 'Greetings...' Or even 'Salutations...' 'Salutations, brethren...' But that's a temptation that must be resisted. Jesus of course was tempted in the desert many times, by Satan, as we know.

And we have a different temptation: to be like religion. To be like all the others, with their antiquated language and their blind belief. That's what the language is for, why it has persisted. Because people venerate time, people sanctify the past. The old religions have power because they are old. But we are not. We are new. And we are not blind. Jesus's temptation – we do not believe it happened. We know the exact probability of it having happened.

She presses a button. On one screen comes up. 'Jesus Tempted by Satan' and an equation... with the answer 10 to power of 3.4.

Below that the biblical number = 4.2 X 10 power of -18.

CONGREGATION. Matthew 3: fifty-four equals six-point-six times ten to the power of minus thirty-four.

EDIE. Which may seem small. But in the quantum universe everything is small; and moreover everything is probable. In the quantum universe, there is no such thing as truth. Only gradations of probability.

CONGREGATION. Truth is probability, probability truth.

EDIE. Someone once said to me that she knows that God does not exist like she knows that stone is hard. But stone is not hard. Stone is energy, stone is dense with movement: it is only hard relative to the sensations our brain processes through the hand. What is the probability that stone might be soft? Soft as water?

*She presses a button. On another screen: 'Water from a Rock'.
An equation and:*

Biblical number = 3.8 x 10 to power of -23.

CONGREGATION. Exodus equals three point eight times ten
to the power of minus twenty-three.

EDIE. So what should I call you, if not brethren? Let me call
you: researchers. That is what we are. We are searching and
re-searching, like scientists do, never settling on a theory as
fact because we know other theories are out there, soon to
emerge. And researchers: we have to face something. These
numbers around me. They all refer to events in the distant
past. The equations have confirmed something: they've
brought us the sacred possible truth, the holy probability. In
these numbers lies hope: lies potential. But potential must
always be about the future not the past. So let's look to some
new numbers. Not about the miracles that have been, but the
miracles that are yet to be. The ones that are... and allow me
here a little antiquated language... foretold.

*Lights down on her. Lights up on the mezzanine area.
HENRY is standing there, where there is a door to the
chapel. If he walked through that door, he would appear on
the balcony of the chapel.*

He holds his phone.

VIRGINIA (*off*). Henry!

*He turns. She enters from the wings. Though she has an
urgent expression, she does not go to him, but stands apart.
TIM enters too, but stands apart.*

HENRY. Well. Fancy meeting you... two... here.

Beat.

You're just in time for Edie's sermon. Or lecture. I think it's
a bit of both.

VIRGINIA. Is it on lattice gauge theory?

HENRY. Yeah. I lied about that.

VIRGINIA. I know.

HENRY. I'm thinking. About whether or not I should go in.

Beat.

Why is Tim here, Virginia?

TIM. I drove her.

HENRY. Oh. I see. Because I assume, Virginia, you'd been drinking...

VIRGINIA. Well. Yes.

HENRY. And halfway through the second bottle your old friend Tim turns up... with some interesting intel about your husband...

TIM. I went to see Virginia because I'm going through... a bad time, Henry. A bad time caused by your... stupid bloody quantum angel.

HENRY. Ah right. I see. *That's* why you chose to drive my wife all the way down here? Revenge.

TIM. No!

VIRGINIA. Well yes. You went on about what a total fucking bitch she is all the way down.

TIM. Okay yes maybe. Because, me, I'm no angel of any sort. So yes, probably, in my mess of shit feelings about all this, some kind of revenge was in the mix.

HENRY. Right.

TIM. So... vis-à-vis my *revenge*... Have you done it, Henry?

HENRY. Done what?

TIM. You told me you were coming here to tell Edie to shut the whole thing down. How's that going?

HENRY (*looks round at the chapel*). Not well. I never did have much authority with my students.

TIM. Henry. Don't let her weave whatever weird magic she holds on you. Because for all her cleverness, she still needs you. To make her fucking... science-religion mongrel sit up and bark. *You're* who gives her – who gives all this – credibility. So… Go in there. Tell her – tell them all – that you think it's bollocks.

HENRY. I don't. Not quite.

TIM. You're a Professor of fucking Physics! Go in there and do what you told me you came here to do! Kill this movement!

HENRY (*beat; holds up phone*). I also told you not to tell my wife where I was. But you can't be trusted, can you, Tim? Certainly not if this recording that I've just listened to is anything to go by.

TIM (*wind out of sails*). Oh… I was hoping you might not have heard that…

HENRY (*of phone*). Took me ages to download. Shit reception here.

Beat. TIM *looks to* VIRGINIA*: help…?*

VIRGINIA. Henry. When that happened… when Tim took Edie out for a drink…

HENRY. Blackmailed her to meet him do you mean?

VIRGINIA. Yes. I'm not saying that wasn't totally cunty…

TIM. Thanks.

VIRGINIA.…but she told him a lot of weird stuff.

TIM. About being abused by her father, about sadistic nuns, all sorts, and then refused to confirm that any of it was true.

HENRY. And…?

VIRGINIA. And I think she might be damaged, Henry. And unstable. Because who does that? I think she might be a psychotic religious fanatic, and the fact that she's young and beautiful and white rather than bearded and brown and waving a black flag is blinding you to that fact. And maybe – for all his idiotic inexcusable behaviour – Tim's right: that she might be using you as a central part of whatever the fuck her psychotic fanatic plan is.

HENRY. Or maybe, she said some extremely off-putting things about herself in order to put someone off. Tim, to be exact.

VIRGINIA. Well. Yes. That is also possi–

HENRY. And here's the thing, Tim. I'm not your mate. Your old mucker. Not any more. And hey: let's none of us pretend you went round to see my wife late at night just to cry on her shoulder.

A glance between TIM *and* VIRGINIA.

VIRGINIA. Sorry, what are you saying exactly?

TIM. For fuck's sake, Henry! Virginia is my… friend. I needed a friend. And – as you've just made perfectly clear – my best male one doesn't want the job any more!

VIRGINIA. Also, Henry… *I* needed one too. I also seem to have lost my best friend.

HENRY (*beat; raises a hand to his forehead*). Yes. Well. I'm trying to hold a lot of cognitive dissonance in my head at the minute. A lot of contradictions. Science, religion… real, not-real – but forgive me if there's one I can't contain. Which is…

Looks to TIM.

predator…

(*To* VIRGINIA.) …friend to women. That's too much. I just don't think a sex addict who abuses his position to prey on young women really believes in the concept of platonic female friends.

Beat.

Do you, Virginia?

TIM. Fuck you, you big Jesus. Fuck off. I can't believe this.

Starts towards the chapel.

Okay. *Someone* needs to call out this crap. I might just go in there and – and – and –

VIRGINIA. Tim. I want… I need to talk to my husband. Alone. Please.

TIM (*deflated*). Okay. I'll wait in the car.

Looks over.

Enjoy your flawlessness, Henry. Enjoy being a god.

He exits. Beat.

VIRGINIA. So… I'm getting a sense here – perhaps I have for a while – that I'm in the way… of whatever it is that's between you and Edie, between you and your… destiny. But still – I think – *you* can't end it. Us. You *need* it to be me. The cause. Because otherwise you're the bad guy. And you, Henry, can never be the bad guy. You have to be the hero. So just like her, in there, just like all religions – you've constructed a story – a fantasy – this thing, about me and Tim – that fits your narrative.

HENRY. It's not a fantasy, Virginia. He loves you. He's always loved you. It's obvious.

VIRGINIA. Maybe. But I don't love him. I love you.

Lights down on them. Up on EDIE. EDIE*'s sermon continuing.*

EDIE. How would you like to win the lottery?

Beat; clicks on monitor.

Not *this* lottery…

Image on screen of lottery winners.

Because that, nice though it would be, is a transient prize. No. The prize that lasts forever. The true winnings. *This* lottery.

Clicks on remote: images of Rapture, Second Coming, etc., onscreen.

To be among the Saved on the Day of Judgement.

Beat.

Well, you can. Not in the wishy-washy way that the Old Church would tell you – by hoping it'll happen at some point in the distant future – no. It can happen, for you, tomorrow.

Here's how. Quantum physics tells us that in an infinite universe, anything is not just possible, but inevitable. Somewhere, everything is happening. So. Let's do the maths, on this inevitability: the Second Coming.

She presses a button. A trumpet sounds. The screens fill with images of apocalypse.

The Book of Revelations tells us there will be seven trumpets. Six of these will coincide with a different disaster: an earthquake, a tsunami, an asteroid collision, a war, a plague, a great woe upon the Earth, and on the seventh, it is the Last Judgement. The world will have melted away, to become the Kingdom of God. So what is the probability of those seven trumpets sounding? Let me show you.

Lights down on her. Lights up on VIRGINIA *and* HENRY *still facing each other.*

HENRY (*after a beat*). You know, the night after the book launch, why I asked you about reading *God's Dice*, Virginia? It's because I've read yours. All of them. Cover to cover.

VIRGINIA. I know.

HENRY. And they're brilliant of course. But they are just saying one thing, over and over again. Something that was said – better – by Philip Larkin. That vast moth-eaten musical brocade created to pretend we never die. That's what he called religion, didn't he?

VIRGINIA. Yes.

HENRY. That seems to be what you're choosing to say again, in a number of different ways. But maybe – maybe – what they're creating here – what Edie's doing here – it isn't moth-eaten. It's new. It's scientific.

VIRGINIA (*nodding*). It's a vast musical brocade made of some kind of new polymer resistant to moths...

HENRY. I'm not sure cynicism helps.

VIRGINIA. I'm joking, Henry. That used to be something we used to do together, a lot. And also... I'm reacting. To you slagging off my books.

HENRY. I'm not –

VIRGINIA. You are. You're angry. Which I understand. We weren't quite as good as we thought at marriage, were we? But I think… there might still be time to fix that.

Beat; she reaches out a hand.

Come home.

Lights down on them. Lights up on EDIE. *New equations on the screen.*

EDIE.…which gives us: six-point-six times ten to the power of minus thirty-four-point-seven-five-eight. That is the probability of all the predictions foretold in Revelations coming true. That tiny number… can win us the lottery.

Beat; she bends down, picks up a box: it looks like a remote receiver of some sort – it has lights on it, perhaps a counter with numbers – and inscribed TGC.

This box contains a capsule of cyanide. For which provision, I thank you, fellow researchers from the chemistry community.

The gas released, were the capsule to break, would kill us all. Opening the box will break the capsule. Tonight, at midnight – in ten minutes from now – it is programmed to open.

Beat.

But don't worry.

She puts the box down in front of her; clicks on screen: and algorithm appears.

Because I have an algorithm. This algorithm is already out there, on the internet – and the box knows about it. And the box will NOT open if the internet registers enough usages – enough hits – of the words…

These come up onscreen, illustrated, hashtagged as they would be on Twitter/Instagram, etc.

…asteroid, tsunami, earthquake, war, woe and Second Coming. I've put in other words just to make sure: apocalypse, four horseman, Jesus, hashtag-end-of-the-world.

Which means that although in many universes, the box will open and we will die, in one universe amongst the ten to the power of thirty-four universes… we will be saved. We will have won the lottery.

Beat: then – to the actual audience, as well as to the congregation…

You don't believe me. You're thinking: this can't possibly be happening. None of this would happen. In reality. Like people do with quantum physics: or, when they see God. Both present a universe of mysterious infinite possibility; which makes it hard, doesn't it, to locate what is and isn't real…?

Lighting change. Back up on VIRGINIA *and* HENRY *outside.*

HENRY. Why don't we have children, Virginia?

VIRGINIA. Henry.

HENRY. No, really why?

VIRGINIA. Please let's not pivot to this now.

She sighs.

All the reasons we talked about, endlessly. Career… timing… fear of making a mistake…

HENRY. Whose career? Whose timing? Whose fear?

VIRGINIA. Both of ours. I thought.

HENRY (*shakes his head*). I think there is maybe something that happens when you have a child. I don't know because we don't have one but… I think it brings with it maybe some kind of transcendence. And I think you don't want there to be transcendence. In life.

VIRGINIA. That's totally wrong. I have no fear of wonder.

HENRY. But you don't ache for it, either, do you, Virginia? You know your great atheist epiphany? When someone asked 'But don't you *want* to believe in God?' – and you felt how much you did want that, and knew immediately that therefore He does not exist, that He is a projection of desire – that person is me.

VIRGINIA. No, it was –

HENRY. Or may as well be. *I* want to believe in God. Or: I want
to believe in *something*. I want transcendence. I am a small
man – a quantum man, if you like – and like all us down here
in the quantum universe we dream of something bigger. We
dream of a *pattern* – a pattern we might make when all us tiny
particles are seen from above. Some – like you – they're so
strong, so self-sufficient – don't need that dream. But I do.

He turns towards the door. He wants to go on. VIRGINIA
looks at him keenly.

VIRGINIA. Perhaps you're right. Perhaps I don't ache for
wonder. Perhaps I'm missing a… spiritual dimension. But
that would be the same reason why I don't ache either for
bullshit.

Beat.

Why did you not tell me you were coming here? If your
purpose was to stop it all, why lie?

HENRY. Because of you. I came here because I couldn't bear to
see *you*… so reduced. So anxious. So depressed. And I felt…
I felt I couldn't tell you that. It seemed… patronising. So
I thought I'd just drive here and tell Edie to wind it up… and
then everything would be better.

VIRGINIA (*nods; beat*). And then… what happened? What
happened to you, Henry? Because… something has.

HENRY (*long beat; sigh; he shakes his head, at the wonder of
it*). I touched her. On the wrist. The face. We touched.
Earlier, tonight. Like you once – a million years ago it seems
– told me not to.

VIRGINIA. Ah…

HENRY. Oh that Ah.

VIRGINIA. What?

HENRY. I used to do that Ah. That all-knowing Ah. Now I don't
think I know enough to make that sound.

Lights down on them. Up on EDIE.

EDIE. So. I sense… fear. I need, I can tell, to convince even the most fervent believers amongst you that this *is* the process that, mathematically, must lead us to Eternal Salvation. Anyone of course is welcome to leave. But before you do, let me see if a smaller miracle – happening right here right now – will convince you to stay – and partake in the bigger one.

She picks up a copy of God's Dice. *She holds it up. It glints in the light.*

As we know, *God's Dice* do not roll for Professor Henry Brook. For all his wisdom, all his insight, he cannot match up the *evidence* in his own book to the obvious conclusion: which is that miracles can, and do, happen. But: the miracle I'm going to present to you is this. Henry Brook will change his mind. Not only that: he will come to us *now*, a changed man.

Presses button: an equation begins formation.

This equation takes into account all the reasons why he would not do that. It gives us a probability of his appearance here, tonight, as approximately one in ten thousand.

Beat.

But of course, what we're also talking about here is a miracle. So if it's a miracle, of course, we need to factor in…

She presses a button: a 'Gd' appears in the equation.

…The God Constant.

She holds up the box.

Lights down on her. Up on HENRY *and* VIRGINIA.

VIRGINIA. Henry… I could have a child. It's not too late. There's a universe in which… we go home now and have our own little miracle.

HENRY. Virginia. You're forty-eight.

VIRGINIA. I believe it's not beyond the bounds of possibility. Given modern science. Certainly the odds are better than a virgin having one… or are they? Has she worked *that* one out?

HENRY. Don't sneer at her. She showed me wonder. She showed me… I'm going to say it, Virginia. She showed me God.

VIRGINIA. It sounds like she showed you her Christian fucking –

HENRY. Don't say it. Please. It's beneath you.

VIRGINIA. Is it? Is it really? When did you get so far above me, Henry?

Beat.

You're right though. It's so stupid and shallow – and not even what I was ever truly worried about, with you and her. It was something else. I think I knew that if you slept with her you would think it was divine. You would feel touched not just by her beautiful young body but by the Holy Spirit. That old, old male sublimation, that basic category error: mistaking rapture for The Rapture.

Beat.

I was half-right, wasn't I? Because you haven't slept with her. Of course you haven't: you're a good husband. Turns out you're so desperate for God you gave your soul to Him for a single touch of her siren skin.

Lights down on them. Lights up inside the chapel.

EDIE. Here we are, researchers, at the edge of our own event horizon. And we can make the miraculous manifest: through prayer. If we pray that Henry Brook will come, we can add this energy – this X, this God Quantum – to the equation.

CONGREGATION. The Word is in the Maths. The Word is in the Maths.

EDIE. The bigger miracle will follow from the smaller.

CONGREGATION. The Word is in the Maths. The Word is in the Maths.

EDIE. Imagine him in your prayer. Think of him, materialising. *Picture* him. *See* him. Because however many billions of universes in which he is not here, *there will be one universe in which Henry Brook is already here* – but only observation, *our* observation, will collapse the wave function – and make him manifest before us.

Lights change. VIRGINIA *and* HENRY *outside as before. But the prayer from inside is audible, and building.*

VIRGINIA. They seem to be building up to something.

HENRY. Yes.

VIRGINIA. Maybe it's ending.

HENRY (*with a hint of sadness*). I don't think so…

VIRGINIA. You're right, of course. Larkin did say it better. But the vast moth-eaten musical brocade isn't the point. Not the one I'm making, or rather, *repeating*, ad nauseam, as you pointed out, in my books. That's all in the subclause: *created to pretend we never die*. That's what all religion is, and you can make it as *rational* and *scientific* and *mothproof* as you like: *it's still a pretence*.

Beat; her voice cracking.

It's still a lie.

HENRY. Maybe. Or maybe what is truth and what is lies isn't as clear as it used to be.

He turns towards the door.

VIRGINIA. Henry… please don't go in there. I have a very bad feeling about it.

HENRY (*beat*). I can't base my decisions on feelings.

Beat.

I'm a scientist.

HENRY *nods. He turns. He's nearly at the door.* HENRY *opens the door to the church. Lights up on the chapel, so both areas are now lit. He goes and stands visible on the higher level.*

Music. HENRY *appears, lit like an angel, the Angel of Revelation.*

CONGREGATION. The Word is in the Maths! THE WORD IS IN THE MATHS!

EDIE (*climbing the stairs triumphantly towards him*). Yes! And the maths, following our words, here, now, has given us a probability of this miracle of...

Presses button: the equation works itself out.

...one.

She smiles at him. Picks up a white robe, waiting there. She hands it to him. He smiles, and puts it on.

The CONGREGATION *continue to chant.* VIRGINIA *watches from outside.*

EDIE *takes his hand and guides him towards the stairs, and his flock. She remains there for a beat, looks to* VIRGINIA.

Bring the chanting down for a moment to hear this final dialogue...

VIRGINIA. Just one question. If your religion is so new and modern and scientific and rational... why the singing? Why the chanting?

A very hard look at EDIE.

Why the robes?

EDIE (*beat; smiles, shrugs*). Showbiz?

Reaction from VIRGINIA. *She shuts the door. Instantly, the lights go down on the chapel, although the chanting can still be heard.*

VIRGINIA *stands there for a moment. She looks towards the door, as if she might open it. And then she turns and walks away.*

Music: Many many fractals become many many religious images, criss-crossed with images of apocalypse, and butterfly wings, to blackout.

End.

A Nick Hern Book

God's Dice first published in Great Britain in 2019 as a paperback original by
Nick Hern Books Limited, The Glasshouse, 49a Goldhawk Road, London
W12 8QP, in association with Avalon and Soho Theatre, London

God's Dice copyright © 2019 David Baddiel

David Baddiel has asserted his moral right to be identified as the author of this
work

Cover photograph of Alan Davies by Helen Maybanks

Designed and typeset by Nick Hern Books, London
Printed in the UK by Mimeo Ltd, Huntingdon, Cambridgeshire PE29 6XX

A CIP catalogue record for this book is available from the British Library

ISBN 978 1 84842 911 6

Woodland
CARBON
www.woodlandcarbon.co.uk
NICK HERN BOOKS
Printed on Carbon Captured paper

www.nickhernbooks.co.uk

facebook.com/nickhernbooks

twitter.com/nickhernbooks